MAKING HOLLYWOOD MAGIC

"My grandmother used to tell me how, whenever [Charlie] Chaplin was in trouble, he would come to the house to have a drink with my grandfather. I can still see pictures of them standing around in the snow, surrounded by old Model As and Model's Ts."
> – Michael Antunez, Third generation Transportation Coordinator, *Pleasantville*

"I was renovating a hacienda in Mexico, so I had goats, chickens and horses running through the set when I heard I'd been nominated."
> – Beth Rubino, Academy Award nominee, *The Cider House Rules*

"I'll never forgot the day I missed an important doctor's appointment because we were trying to capture a twenty-eight foot boa constrictor that had gotten loose and wrapped itself around my leg. When I told the doctor why I'd missed the appointment, he said, 'That has to be true. No one could make it up.'"
> – Larry Needham, Special Effects Technician

"We would get together and visualize everything, asking ourselves, if we were Pilgrims… How would we build furniture? That wasn't easy since the Pilgrims didn't have a lumber yard!"
> – Loren Nickloff, Propmaker, *Erin Brockovich*

"Since Gepetto takes place in the 1800's, pre-industrial revolution, there were no high grade alloys or aluminum. They had only forged metals – brass, tin and steel. Everything had to have that nice Old World flavor but still have the incredible craftsmanship of the best toy maker in the land, which was Gepetto's legacy."
> – David Scott, Property Master

"We rented a Doughboy pool, put it on a stage and built a boathouse around it. We put algae and plastic on the bottom of the pool so it wouldn't look like a pool, and when we shot it, nobody could tell that the boat wasn't on an actual lake."
> – John Kersey, Construction Coordinator

"When they first decided they were going to start letting women in, and I was working as a 'lead man' for various decorators…They put a tool belt on me, had me take off my makeup, and dressed me in clothes from the army/navy surplus store."
> – Rochelle Moser, Set Decorator

"The tricky thing about decorating and designing is that you have to be careful with your inclination to make everything beautiful. In a world where nothing is perfect, it can sometimes detract from the story."
> – Denise Pizzini, Production Designer

MAKING HOLLYWOOD MAGIC
Secrets of Studio Work

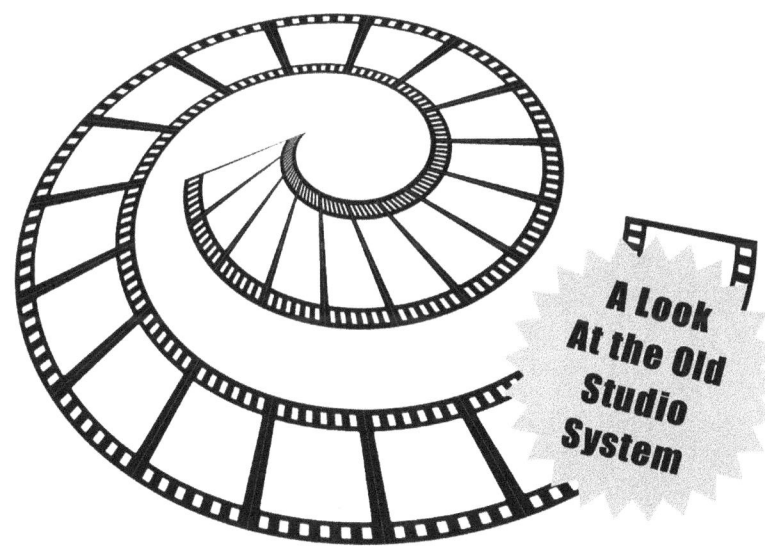

A Look At the Old Studio System

VIVIEN COOPER

Foreword by Beverly Garland, Star of 41 feature films and 700 TV Shows
Afterword by John Villarino, Past President of IATSE Local 44

BearManor Media
2022

Making Hollywood Magic: Secrets of Studio Work

© 2022 Vivien Cooper

All rights reserved.

No portion of this publication may be reproduced, stored, and/or copied electronically (except for academic use as a source), nor transmitted in any form or by any means without the prior written permission of the publisher and/or author.

Photos courtesy of John Villarino.
Jaws photos courtesy of Larry Needham.

Published in the United States of America by:

BearManor Media
1317 Edgewater Dr #110
Orlando FL 32804

bearmanormedia.com

Printed in the United States.

Interior design by Sue Chidester Scott and Cheryl Sealy,
Golden Monarch Graphics

Book Consultant: Flo Selfman, Selfman & Others, PR/<arketing

Cover by John Teehan

ISBN—978-1-62933-916-0

*This book is dedicated to my first hero,
Special Effects Technician
Lawrence "Larry" Needham,
(or Dad, as I call him).*

Table of Contents

Foreword by Beverly Garland ....

Introduction ....

Chapter 1 The Turning Point: The Road to Studio Work 1

Chapter 2 The Perfect Marriage:
Career Matches Made In Heaven 21

Chapter 3 Rush Hour: The Long Hours and Demanding
Schedules Behind The Glamour 49

Chapter 4 Once Upon A Time In America:
Work Begins With The Story..63

Chapter 5 Mission Impossible: Tricks Of The Trade 78

Chapter 6 The Twilight Zone: Out Of The Ordinary 104

Chapter 7 The A-Team: Meet The Crews 130

Chapter 8 Back To The Future: The Changing Face
Of Studio Work..147

Chapter 9 As Good As It Gets:
The Little (And Big) Rewards 165

Chapter 10 It's A Wonderful Life: Reflections From Retirees 188

Afterword by John Villarino, Construction Coordinator and Past
    President of I.A.T.S.E. Local 44 212

Lastword 215

Acknowledgments 218

Index 221

About the Author 232

"To me, this life is like being a circus roustabout. You go to a town, put up the tent, invite everybody in, and then tear it all down and move on."

~ John Villarino, former President,
IATSE Local 44

Foreword

During acceptance speeches at the Oscars and Emmys, among the many people who are thanked with very genuine sincerity by actors is a group of co-workers the audience at home knows little about and very rarely sees – the crew.

I am an actress, just a player in the fast world of make-believe. However, before I can do my job, the canvas needs to be in place. I need the painting, the picture, the color, and the background.

Without the crew – also known as "below-the-line personnel" – my job is impossible to do. They help me create what my imagination envisions. Their work is fascinating.

The craftspeople in my 41 movies and nearly 700 television shows became part of my makeup. They set the scene, from a Western street, to the native village going up in flames; from the snow falling at a stagecoach stop, to the alligator in the swamp I must squirm through; and the New York City street and park that I run through at midnight.

Actors rely on the set builders, set decorators, prop masters, special effects technicians and propmakers, painters, groomsmen, costumers, lighting directors, hair and makeup stylists, stunt people, stage managers, motion picture drivers and everyone who works behind the scenes. Without them, actors would really be nothing.

They teach actors everything: I learned the correct way to shoot a gun, how to execute a karate kick, how to survive the clutches of a boa constrictor that was wrapped around me, and how to escape from a burning building without getting burned.

And when the director surprises an actress saying, "Today you must look exactly the same as when we started this scene *twelve days ago,*" it is the craftspeople working with makeup, hair and costumes who perform the magic.

Good actors understand that we are just one of many parts of a vast production team that creates the whole picture. And we understand that the main reason actors get all the publicity, and sometimes become stars, is because the audience sees just them.

Audiences do not see the people actors depend upon to make them stars. But their work is very visible on the screen. The next time you watch a movie or a television show, look beyond the actor. There is so much more than normally meets the eye.

– Beverly Garland
Star of 41 Feature Films and 700 TV Programs

Introduction

Have you ever turned on the television set, and wondered who made the living room on your favorite show look just like your Aunt Claire's house? Or marveled at how you totally believed you were living in a bygone age, as you enjoyed a treasured movie that takes place in another period in time? Watching a car go over a bridge, head first into a lake, haven't you ever wondered how they did that without killing the actors behind the wheel of the car?

Whenever you see an actor rolling around on fire after a building has exploded and blown sky high, there's a special effects crew you never see. Every time a gangster whips out a cigar and then lights it with the only kind of lighter you could possibly imagine him picking up, there's a property master and his crew at work. Can you imagine Cinderella without her glass slippers and her carriage? You can thank the property department.

And that bridge the car went over? Did you assume it was just a bridge that already existed in some city somewhere? Set construction crews do build bridges – literally and symbolically – and they may build everything from the houses for your favorite sitcom to a massive amusement park. Then set decoration and set dressing crews come in, and fill in all the little touches that turn that house into the home that really does feel like the one in which you grew up.

These are what are known in the industry as "below the line" studio workers.

Who are these workers? How did they get their jobs? What is it like to work outside of corporate America, right in the middle of the movie studios?

The best way to explain what it means to work below the line is this – in the world of film production, there is a line drawn between actors, writers, producers, and directors on one hand, and all other craftspeople on the other. Why is that distinction made? Not surprisingly, it all comes down to money – specifically, budgets.

It is rumored that it all started when someone needed to figure out a way to separate the people on a film who have negotiable salaries and possible profit participation – "above the line" personnel – from those who don't – "below-the-line" personnel. You see, only by first calculating what everyone else is going to earn on a movie, can you figure out what you have left over to allocate for salaries, and profit participation of the actors, writers, director, and producers.

As you may have read in movie magazines and tabloids, the salaries of directors, producers, writers, and actors are always changing, and always unpredictable. Who knows what "A-list" actors are going to make on their next film? Or sought-after directors? It's hard to say, and a lot depends on how well their last film or TV show did. Then when you throw in the fact that they may have a piece of the show's profits on top of the fee they earn, it really gets sticky.

But what can be predicted with some certainty is what will have to be paid below the line, because, for the most part, those workers have fixed salaries. Then it becomes clear how much there is to play with, in negotiating with everyone else.

In other words, imagine you're going to a farmer's market with five dollars in your pocket and you need to come home with an assortment of apples and oranges. And you know that every week, the apples cost the same amount, but you have to negotiate with the vendors on the price of the oranges – because the prices are always changing. You would first figure out, okay, I need ten apples and that's two dollars. That means I have three dollars left to spend on however many oranges that will buy.

Plenty is known about the actors we love. Even other above-the-line personalities have become celebrities in their own right, and there are plenty of magazines and books that you can pick up any day of the week to read about their work and their lives. Most of us know very little about the vast groups of workers that are responsible for the set construction, set decoration, property, or special effects. And most of us know even less about what it is like to work in the highly insular world that lies beyond the front gate of a movie or television studio.

Making Hollywood Magic – Secrets of Studio Work is a compilation of profiles of the unsung heroes that make television shows and films. It is also a stroll around the world of the movie and TV set, giving you a guided, personal, first-hand look at what it is like to work below the line.

The workers profiled here may not get to see their name in lights, enjoy media attention, or out-of-the-ballpark financial rewards – but without them, there would be no television shows or movies.

Without them, there would be no sets to determine the mood and tone of a movie or television show – no floors, walls, or structures built to order – and movie companies would be forced to use whatever building, structure, or forest they could find.

If the script called for it to be raining or snowing outside, actors would have to stop in the middle of their lines to point out those facts to their audience – because there would be no seamless method of conveying those things without special effects.

Actors would have no furniture upon which to sit, jump, stand, lie down, or make love during a scene; and when they picked up a talking shoe, or their hat or gun, the audience would have to imagine what they were holding because there would be no props. In short, the workers profiled in this book are not only indispensable, but without their extensive expertise and highly honed crafts, television and film today would be nothing more than open-air theater, where all but the actors and their lines was left to the imagination.

Imagine you were given carte blanche to walk around the sets, meet the workers, eavesdrop as they talked to each other, and ask them questions about their work and their lives. This dream came true for me. For a period of a year and a half, I did nothing but talk to and write about this particular group of workers.

As you read, you may wish so-and-so had talked more about this, or so-and-so had talked more about that, but what one person doesn't mention, someone else will. Even though I don't give you a blow-by-blow detailing of every single thing these workers do and don't do in the course of a day, you will get a look at studio work in the workers' own words, talking about what is meaningful and interesting to them. In this book, you get to hear the workers talk about their crafts and their lives in the context of whatever show they happened to be on when I wrote the story.

So, if you stay 'til the end, stick it out for the whole story, hopefully, by the time you close the book, all your questions will have been answered. More than that, you'll have a pretty good feeling for what studio work is all about.

In order to talk about every single thing a set decorator or construction coordinator might or might not do, for example, I'd have to be talking to you theoretically because no one is doing everything their job might require all at the same time. On some shows, they might be flexing this muscle, while a different show might call for them to use a whole different set of tools.

Also, all of the workers in this particular book just happen to belong to a union, so talking about what each craftsperson does and doesn't do would turn this book into a very complicated, very technical manual. You may think I'm exaggerating, but any time labor unions are involved, there are very specific rules and laws that must be followed to the letter, as to what workers do, and don't do. For example, worker A might be allowed to pick up a hammer, a saw, and a wrench, but under no circumstances can he ever touch a paint brush. Or, worker B can make smoke and fire but he can't touch a couch – or a broom. If by the time you've finished reading, you still have unanswered questions about what is involved in pursuing a career in any of the fields discussed in this book, you might want to check out the website for the International Alliance of Theatrical and Stage Employees (I.A.T.S.E.) or the website for Teamsters Local 399.

Written with cooperation from the workers, most of these profiles were stories that first appeared in print in film industry union newsletters from the spring of 1999 through the summer of 2000. These stories appear revised from the original format. Please keep in mind as you're reading that what may have been true in 1999 or the year 2000 may not be true today. Shows they thought were going to be a smash may never have taken off, other shows may have run their course or been cancelled, or the show may still be running but the crews they talk about may have changed.

In this book, I focus on four groups of below-the-line workers, and the motion picture drivers. These workers have in common the fact that their work focuses on the sets, environments, atmosphere and props that actors rely upon, as opposed, for example, to costume designers and makeup artists whose work focuses on the appearance of the actors themselves.

Now, at this point you may be asking yourself who I am and why I should be the one writing this book. Well, like many of the workers you're about to meet, I just happened to be in the right place at the right time. It started when I was a little girl and my mother became re-married, to a man named Larry Needham, who went on to become a special effects technician for the movie studios.

For me, growing up with a dad who worked in the movie studios meant having him leave at the crack of dawn, and waiting for him to come home, exhausted. Sometimes he would leave for weeks at a time "on location." I can't remember the number of times Dad came home with something on his body broken, burned, or bent. I'll never forget the day he lost half his thumb.

Or the day the ringing in his ears started – and never stopped.

On the lighter and brighter side, it also meant that when he was laid off, there was still food on the table (thanks to the union). And it meant I got to follow my dad around the set of "The Iron Horse," and that he was able to arrange for me to spend a whole day on the set with Rod Serling ("The Twilight Zone" is my all-time favorite show). It meant he could fix anything, and I mean anything, that broke – often with nothing more than duct tape (much to my mother's horror – duct tape isn't pretty!). I remember Dad bringing home shark's tooth necklaces when he was working on the *Jaws* movies, and always bringing home a good story about life on the set.

I asked my brother, Ray [Campbell], what he remembered growing up with Dad.

"When I was a kid," Ray recalls, "it was always neat to tell my friends that my dad did the 'effects' for shows like 'Bewitched,' 'I Dream of Jeannie,' and 'My Favorite Martian.' Later, as a Universal Studios Tour Guide, my groups used to 'ooh' and 'aah' when I told them that he built the sharks for *Jaws*."

With a total of five kids in the house, that movie studio paycheck made all the difference in the world. And it brought into our home a world very few people knew much about. It was the world we saw on the TV set. And it was the world we saw when we walked into the local movie theater, got cozy in our seats, and looked up at that huge screen with feelings I still have today – pure excitement, anticipation and awe.

More than that, the movies have always given me hope. When I sit down and watch a film, I become part of a larger fabric. Watching what others go through on this incredible journey we call life touches me in many ways – there are times it inspires me and times it disturbs me. Sometimes TV and movies tickle me, sometimes they make me cry. They always make me reflect and think. And like I said, they always give me hope.

This book will give you insight, information and details about TV and filmmaking that you couldn't discover on your own. It is my hope that the more you know about movies and television shows, the more you will enjoy them.

Have fun. God knows, I did.

1
The Turning Point
The Road to Studio Work

So, how do you get into studio work, anyway? For some, the road to the studios was a straight line from Point A to Point B, and every door swung open as if by magic. For others, their career path had more twists and turns than a Hollywood car chase.

Garrett Lewis, Set Decorator
Panic Room, I Am Sam, Fun with Dick and Jane, among others

Academy Award Nominations:
1989, Nominated (shared), Best Art Direction – Set Decoration, ***Beaches***
1990, Nominated (shared), Best Art Direction – Set Decoration, ***Glory***
1992, Nominated (shared), Best Art Direction – Set Decoration, ***Hook***
1993, Nominated (shared), Best Art Direction – Set Decoration, ***Dracula***

Emmy Award Nominations:
2000, Nominated (shared), Outstanding Art Direction for a Miniseries, Movie or a Special, ***Gepetto***

Academy and Emmy Award-nominated Set Decorator Garrett Lewis now works behind the scenes, creating the canvas upon which the actors express themselves, but he began his life in show biz as a singer, dancer, and actor. Prior to that, the St. Louis native majored in art.

He was expecting to follow the commercial design path but happened to be dating a girl in a modern dance group that needed male dancers. He joined, found he had an unexpected aptitude for dance, and was discovered by a famous choreographer.

Lewis was asked to go to Kansas City and ended up dancing for the summer. Figuring he'd go home at the end of the summer, he was told, "If you go to New York, you'll get work in a minute." He did, and within two weeks was on Broadway, dancing in

My Fair Lady. He later co-starred with Carol Channing in *Hello Dolly*.

Lewis credits Herbert Ross, who was married to Lewis's agent, with getting him into this side of the industry. The Rosses had just bought a house in Los Angeles, after relocating from New York. They asked Lewis to decorate their house, which led to interior design work on homes for Barry Diller, Barbra Streisand and other Hollywood notables.

While Garrett Lewis was decorating homes, Herbert Ross was directing *The Turning Point* and asked the artist to consult on the right look for the theater in which the character, Nora, played by Anne Bancroft, performs. After that, Ross went on to do *California Suite*, on which Lewis again served as a visual consultant. Ray Stark, the producer of that film, arranged for him to get another Warner Bros. project, a *Star Wars* Holiday Special.

Lewis remembers, "He gave me my time and made it possible for me to join the union."

Virtually everything he has touched since then has turned to gold.

"*Dracula* was an interesting research project," he recalls, "bringing the audience from fifteenth century Romania up to the turn of the century. And *Glory* taught me so much more about the Civil War than I'd ever known before."

The decorator says *Misery* was a challenge because of "the constraints of having almost the entire movie take place in the bedroom, knowing it would be seen over and over. The choices were very specific."

"Whether, like in Wendy's bedroom in *Hook*, I fill a room with memories and pictures or eliminate everything but a small picture; or whether I walk into an existing building and completely change the environment like I did on *Pretty Woman*, choices are what my job is all about," said the celebrated set decorator whose award-nominated work behind the scenes almost wasn't.

Laurie C. Dalton, Property Master
Greener Mountains, "That '80s Show," "My So-Called Life,"
among others

Before she moved to Los Angeles, Laurie Dalton decided that maybe she wasn't cut out to be a high school teacher after all, so she got out her cookie cutter and opened the Santa Barbara Cookie Company.

She had been teaching school in Oxnard for a year on a government-funded project for "upward bound, low income kids" and the funding got cancelled, so Dalton shelved her teaching credentials and picked up an apron.

"I was spoiled by having a small class and I just couldn't face thirty kids every single day," she explains.

While baking for a living, Dalton played guitar in a local band.

"Our band opened for the Kinks and The Blasters and I thought my career would be in music," she remembers. "Then my band broke up. And then I got tired of the bakery business."

"About that time, a friend of mine told me she was going to do a movie in Arizona, and suggested I go along with her and try to get into the Art Department," Dalton reports.

She ended up getting a job on that film as a Producer's Assistant, but spent her down time with her friend, Katie Carmichael, an Assistant Property Master.

"I thought what she was doing was so cool, and it didn't take long for me to figure out that it was exactly what I wanted to do," says the former teacher and baker.

Dalton's career to date has focused mostly on one-hour television dramas, including the smash hit "Beverly Hills 90210" and "My So-Called Life."

According to Dalton, "'Beverly Hills 90210' was like a meteor ride. The first year, everyone thought the show was going to be a loser. Then, suddenly, the summer after it had aired for a whole season, the world just went crazy over it, and people were asking me for my autograph."

Pedro Zapata, Motion Picture Drive
[worked on: **"Brutally Normal," "Felicity,"** among others]

"I said I wasn't interested in the movie business. But as soon as I took the job, I could see that it was gorgeous," relates Pedro Zapata, Motion Picture Driver.

Growing up in Puerto Rico, Zapata never dreamed he would end up in Hollywood. And he certainly never saw himself driving a motor home for Richard Pryor.

Landing in the Big Apple when he first emigrated to America, Zapata quickly saw the opportunities available, and the quality of life afforded by belonging to a union.

The former member of New York's Handyman's Union Local 42 says, "Never take a job without the union. You'll have no protection. They'll fire you if they feel like it, and you'll be underpaid with no benefits. I love the union – good jobs, good pay, good benefits. It's a much better way to earn a living."

While taking in the sights and sounds of New York City, he worked for the Airport Transit Bus Company – which is when he first discovered life as a Teamster. When that job had run its course, he was asked if he wanted to work for the studios.

"I've loved every minute of it," he recalls. "It's great mingling with everyone, from the people you work with, to the directors and the producers and the stars."

Rubbing elbows with the stars came after years of elbow grease. Earning four dollars an hour to start, Zapata joined Teamsters Local 399 in 1972, and went to work in the service department. Getting the vehicles spic and span for the next day's shoot kept him busy for three years. Next stop: tram driver for the tours.

The driver remembers, "I did that for three or four years and then I decided it was time to make some money, so I went to work on the shows. I ended up under contract to Richard Pryor, a really wonderful man."

As time rolls by, Zapata forges close ties with those he works with on shows like "Brutally Normal." When I spoke with him last, the motion picture driver was at work on the popular drama "Felicity." He says the crew was filled with friends who had become like family. And Zapata appreciates family.

When we spoke, he was only two years away from retirement, and was dreaming about where his road might lead him.

Now quite at home in the land of opportunity, he says. " I'm a good cook. Maybe I'll open a little Puerto Rican Restaurant."

With his passion for living, Zapata is sure to put sizzle and spice into whatever he chooses to do.

Ryan Effner
Propmaker: *She's All That*
Swing Gang: *Never Too Young to Die*
Special Effects: *A Nightmare On Elm Street: The Dream Child*
(among others)

Nowhere is the phrase "Don't call us, we'll call you" more prevalent than in the entertainment industry. But, as Ryan Effner proved, for every closed door policy, there is an open window — if you just know where to find it and how to slip through.

Growing up in Michigan, Effner developed a relationship with a hammer and nails while building a couple of houses with his father. One in particular stands out in his memory. When Effner's grandfather's farm burned down right on the cusp of retirement, Effner and his father built a house on their property for him.

"For one year before I moved to California, it was really nice to have three generations on the same property," reports Effner. "Anyway, it was from that experience that I ended up doing construction. It had always been meaningful work for me."

Ryan Effner's introduction to studio carpentry did not follow the usual plot lines. The way the story typically goes, an aspiring actor works behind the scenes while awaiting his break in front of the camera. Effner, on the other hand, was pursuing his ambition to act and write, and toward those ends was working in front of the camera as an extra. Extra work being what it is — hours and hours of standing around — he volunteered to lend a hand to the carpenters working next door. A couple of months later when he was looking for a gig, he walked into the same non-union movie house, where they remembered him and put him to work.

Effner found himself working on the *Nightmare On Elm Street* films, doing propmaking and mechanical special effects. About halfway through *Nightmare On Elm Street 4,* the maker of the razor gloves so pivotal to those films moved on, and gave the templates to Effner. A long way from home, the grandson of a Michigan farmer found himself making the famous *Nightmare On Elm Street* gloves.

Work for New Line Cinema led to more television shows and features, including *Graveyard Shift*, on which he had the chance to join the union. Effner got his feet wet working on the massive aquarium tank for *Free Willy*.

In 1989, after working on *Bugsy*, Effner wanted a permanent place at Paramount Studios. So, every morning for three weeks, he arrived at 5:45 a.m. And every morning they told him to go away. They promised to call him in a couple of weeks. Whenever they would tell him, "We'll call you," he would simply say, "Bye! I'll see you tomorrow."

Remembering his persistence, Effner laughs, saying, "I figured that by showing up every morning, they would know that, number one, I had a good attitude, and number two, I could show up for work on time. That was two out of three, so the only thing left to prove was that I really could do propmaking."

The Turning Point: The Road to Studio Work

The propmaker has definitely traveled a circuitous route to his dreams, from center stage as an actor to studio work behind the scenes. The multi-talented Effner also wrote, directed, and acted in a semi-autobiographical film entitled *If Men Could Talk*. When it came time to do his own film, he was overwhelmed by the support he received — payback for pitching in to help out a bunch of carpenters so many years ago.

"It was such a wonderful experience making my first feature film. Panavision donated cameras, Kodak donated all the film stock, and thirty-six SAG actors worked on full deferments. I couldn't believe it," he says, gratefully.

Effner's story is proof positive that there are many ways to get from Point A to Point B, and not all of them run in a straight line.

Stanford Davis, Motion Picture Driver
Liberty Stands Still, Blade, White Men Can't Jump, among others

Motion Picture Driver Stanford Davis was almost ten years old before he ever set eyes on a car.

Growing up in the Bahamas, where the pace was much more relaxed and breezy, it was not unusual for entire weeks to pass between one automobile sighting and the next. The thought that he would someday earn his living as a driver – in the motion picture industry, of all places – would have seemed very far-fetched.

He remembers, "I always figured I'd end up in the fishing or tourism industry, but I don't really like domestic work and I hate being confined. That's why I love driving so much – instead of being stuck in an office, I'm out in the open meeting people. I really enjoy the freedom."

In 1972, *Day of the Dolphins* was filming in the Bahamas, and hiring locals for the construction crew, so they put Davis to work building sets.

As things began to slow down, he went to another island to pick up work. When he returned to the first island to enjoy the Christmas holiday, he discovered that someone had been looking for him. It was the construction foreman, who moved Davis out of construction, and jump-started his career in transportation.

Shortly thereafter, Walter Freitas, who became like a father to Davis, asked him if he wanted to try to work in the States, giving him a deadline to get a passport. The next thing he knew, he was in Miami, along with all the production vehicles that had been shipped back home on barges. Freitas pointed to a crew van and told him, "You're driving this back to California."

"I couldn't believe it," Davis remembers, with a laugh. "On the one hand, I was kind of excited. On the other hand, I had just come from an island where there is only one lane of cars, and I was looking at four or five lanes here. I was also overwhelmed by the number of people in Miami – it was incredible. On my island, everybody knew each other."

Somehow, the islander got himself and the van safely home to Hollywood, where he began a driving career that has never been short on adventure. One time in New Mexico, just outside of Santa Fe, the camera was a mile and a half from the truck when Davis noticed some menacing-looking storm clouds on the horizon.

The crew was sitting around eating lunch as he watched the clouds grow blacker, so Davis urged, "We better get the equipment off the hill."

When they got in the van it was only sprinkling but before they had gone a quarter of a mile, a wall of water was coming straight at them.

"We barely made it out of there alive," he remembers, shaking his head, and chuckling at the memory.

Another memorable moment took place on location in Texas, when the crew had to find a way to keep their equipment out of sight, in order to accommodate a shot that spanned 365 degrees. So they hid it in a ravine. When the shot was over, it took a big rig tow truck and five hundred feet of cable to drag the equipment back onto level ground.

"It has all been a wonderful experience," he relates, "and there is nothing I would do any differently. I love this industry, and when I hit the peaks and valleys, I just try to ride with the flow."

While Davis has adapted to life in the big city, and enjoyed his career tremendously, the man who grew up in the Bahamas has never lost sight of his traditional values. He believes in working hard, and giving equal attention and energy to everyone for whom he works, regardless of their status. And he has built his reputation that way, as a man who lives by the Golden Rule. He's very clear on his priorities, and for Davis, family comes first. Between productions, he spends as much quality time with his wife and children as possible, and when he does travel, he makes sure his loved ones are never more than four or five days behind him.

He visits the Bahamas once a year, and hopes to someday return to the island lifestyle he left behind so many years ago. When he's on the road, living in high rise hotels, his mind sometimes wanders to the free-standing island houses of his youth. And he longs for the wide open spaces and tropical rhythms. But for Stanford Davis, who has developed the adaptability that allows him to be comfortable wherever he may find himself, home is where the heart is.

"When I am with the ones I love, I try to enjoy every minute. Because none of us knows what the future may hold. Live life, enjoy it, treat people the way I like to be treated – that's my motto."

John Hartigan
Special Effects Director: *In Good Company*
Special Effects Coordinator: *American Beauty, Gepetto*
(among others)

John Hartigan often ponders the unlikelihood of his career path. After being raised in upstate New York, he attended college in North Carolina, studying hotel and restaurant management. Planning to travel the world and eventually seek a management position with a large hotel chain, he was sidetracked by a California-bound cousin, who happened to have a pretty friend of hers along for the ride.

In one of those strange turns the road of life often takes, the New Yorker put his hotel and restaurant ambitions aside, and followed his cousin and her friend out to California. Before long, his cousin was dating someone in special effects, and the seed that would eventually sprout into a full-blown career was planted in Hartigan's mind.

"When I got here, I was having such a great time that after about a month and a half, I thought maybe I'd try to get into the studios," he recalls. "I was young and enjoying myself, and I didn't really want to go back to New York."

Hartigan persisted in his efforts to join the biz, and eventually landed work at CBS on *Raise the Titanic* and *The Muppet Movie*.

On *Gepetto*, actors flying through sets, acrobats spinning in the air, and dance floors rotating at the flip of a switch were all in a day's work for John Hartigan.

"A lot of the set pieces had to move, spin, and turn on that show," he explains. "We even had a roller coaster where Pinocchio rides around, enters a machine at the end of the ride, and changes into a donkey."

With so many wonderful shows to his credit, the industry veteran is obviously happy with his decision to make California and the film industry his home.

He sums it all up with a smile, saying, "It's such a wonderful way to make a living, because every day you're doing something different. In this business, everything is constantly changing."

Michael Antunez
Transportation Captain: *Blue Streak*
Transportation Coordinator: *Pleasantville, Crimson Tide*
(among others)

Looking back over his life in the industry, Michael Antunez says that what he loves the most are the relationships he has had a chance to build.

"The only problem is that you end up working with these different guys for months or even a year sometimes, and you get really close. And then the show ends and the crew splits up. So you become like family, but then you rarely get to see each other."

The third generation Transportation Coordinator values family, and he is living proof that you can feel the pull of family tradition without even knowing your kin.

As a child, all that he knew of the family business he learned from stories and photographs. As "Charlie Chaplin's transportation man," his grandfather, Frank Antunez, was a legend.

"My grandmother used to tell me how, whenever Chaplin was in trouble, he would come to the house to have a drink with my grandfather. I can still see pictures of them standing around in the snow, surrounded by old Model A's and Model's T's."

Michael Antunez never did get to meet his granddad, who passed away before he was born, and he would turn nineteen years old before he first shook hands with his dad, James (Jimmy)

Antunez. Long before that meeting, the younger Antunez had his future all mapped out. He loved to draw, and concentrated on drafting courses in junior college.

"I had always wanted to do drawing and engineering, but being a draftsman turned out to be repetitive and monotonous. There I was, wearing a suit and tie, working as a structural design draftsman, but I felt claustrophobic being inside all day. Being locked away in an office with a bunch of guys sitting around a drawing board just wasn't cutting it," he recalls.

So he took a leave of absence to reconsider his life. It wasn't long before he had grease under his fingernails, and his head under the hood at the body shop co-owned by his uncle and his father.

When his dad told him of openings, he started to take sporadic jobs in studio transportation. He remained reluctant to jump into the business, preferring the nuts and bolts of mechanics.

"I really enjoyed working at the body shop, but there's something that draws you into the entertainment business," he muses. "You do a little bit, then a little bit more, and then you realize how much you like the people. The environment is a lot of fun."

Antunez had been working as a coordinator since 1979, when his dad had to take a pass on a picture, and passed it along to him. He says that over the years, the amount of equipment everyone carries has quadrupled to where they use four trucks where they used to need only one. He has also watched the studio system change from the days when producers and directors made a schedule and everyone stuck to it.

"Now it's a whole different mentality," he reports. "Everyone has cell phones, pagers, and fax machines. Which means they can reach you twenty-four hours a day. That technology allows them to constantly change their minds, so things now change minute by minute. You run on a wing and a prayer."

Before James Antunez's death in 1998, father and son forged a close bond. After Tony Burella, Sr. gave him his first opportunity to captain on the series "CHIPS," Michael Antunez had a chance to work with his father.

"We worked together on some independents and he taught me a great deal. Even though we are from different generations and have different ways of doing things, I'll always be grateful for everything he taught me. I miss him terribly."

When we talked, he was at work on two features, *Metal God* and *Pearl Harbor*. Michael Antunez works twelve or more hours a day but always makes his sons a priority, spending as much time with them as possible.

Lessons learned in his own life have taught Michael Antunez his priorities, and he takes some comfort in knowing that even when you don't see each other, family ties transcend all barriers.

2

The Perfect Marriage
Career Matches Made In Heaven

For plenty of people, the word "happiness" and the word "work" just don't go together.

Here are a few of the lucky ones, who seem to have been born to their positions. These workers have made the perfect marriage at work. From the time they were young, everything seemed to point to their ending up in the movie studios – right where they belong.

Rochelle Moser, Set Decorator
"3rd Rock From the Sun," "The New WKRP in Cincinnati," "Remington Steele," among others

Emmy Award Nominations:
1995, Won (shared), Outstanding Individual Achievement
in Art Direction for a Series, **"Cybill"**
1996, Nominated (shared), Outstanding Individual Achievement
in Art Direction for a Series, **"Cybill"**

Set Decorator Rochelle Moser happened to be in the right place at a time when the male-dominated movie industry began to relax its borders to include the female population.

"When they first decided they were going to start letting women in, and I was working as a 'lead man' for various decorators, they tried to make me look inconspicuous so I could fit in with all the men. They put a tool belt on me, had me take off my make-up, and dressed me in clothes from the army/navy surplus store," Moser recalls good-naturedly.

The head of personnel at Universal was the one who opened the window of opportunity for Moser, thanks to shared lunch breaks in the commissary while she was working in another department at the studio.

As a little girl from Brooklyn, who moved west with her parents when she was eight years old, Moser had always been creatively oriented. After marrying young and living in Italy for a couple of years, the New Yorker returned to the States, and began to do interior design for various businesses and homes.

It was a serendipitous moment during her stint as an interior designer that steered her toward the movie biz. One of her clients noticed that her sensibilities were a little bit left of center, and mentioned that she might want to consider doing sets.

"My approach to design was somewhat unusual," Moser admits.

Following her years as a "lead man," "The Dukes of Hazzard" very gently broke her into set decoration. She calls the experience "so easygoing, it was a ball," and notes that had she been assigned to a high-tech show her first time out of the gate, she would have been scared to death.

Moser worked on "Cybill" and also decorated the pilots for "Remington Steele" and "Third Rock From The Sun." If "Cybill" was the depiction of modern day urbanity, "Thanks," starring Cloris Leachman, Kristen Nelson and Tim Dutton, was the polar opposite.

"The décor is all authentic and the comedy is so funny, it's almost a farce," notes the decorator.

One scene in the Pilgrim-based "Thanks" has the mother going crazy cooking things over the stove, while the daughter says, "Maybe someday they'll come up with a flat cooking surface, so you can do other things while the food is cooking."

Doing an immense amount of research on the era, Moser and her team made some interesting discoveries about the way the Pilgrims lived.

"It's amazing that any of us are alive today, when you consider the poor health conditions they suffered, and the fact that they did things like building fireplaces out of wood," Moser jokes. "They lost fifty percent of the population the first year after the Mayflower came over."

Courtney Jackson
Production Designer: *Nine Lives*
Property Master: *"Angel"*
Assistant Property Master: *Confessions of a Dangerous Mind*
(among others)

As an art history major at Cal State Northridge, Courtney Jackson figured she would probably find herself working in an art gallery or museum – until her brother, an assistant A.D., took her under his wing. She began working first as a set dresser, but everything clicked when she found the world of props.

"Working in props is so collaborative, you can actually see your work as it's happening," she says, delighted.

Disney's *The Wonderful Ice Cream Suit,* with Joe Mantegna and Edward James Olmos, gave the property master her entry into the union in 1997. She went on to work on "Angel," the spin-off to "Buffy The Vampire Slayer" on which she was property assistant.

While working on famed director Alfonso Arau's *Picking Up The Pieces*, Jackson said, "Anything is possible in Arau's world. It's not about practicality. It's never an issue of, well, we only have this much time or this much money. When you're working with him, it's possible until it's proven to be impossible."

It was the first time Jackson had worked with Woody Allen, and she says she found it utterly remarkable that he would take the role of actor, and completely defer to Arau as the director.

"Alfonso would ask him what he wanted, and you couldn't believe he didn't have an opinion," she remembers, incredulous. "Even with actors who aren't directors, you rarely see that happen."

Alfonso Arau's curious dark comedy turned out to be very hands-on for the property master.

"*Picking Up The Pieces* was real prop-intensive because the mayor of the town decides there's money to be made if he exploits the fact that a hand is creating miracles. So we had lights that looked like fingers, a cigarette lighter shaped like a thumb, and bendable hand keychains. We even had to come up with piñatas, shaped like hands that spilled hand-shaped candy."

In Arau's film filled with Latin American imagery, Jackson thoroughly enjoyed the task of bringing all the symbolism to life.

"Arau's creativity was always flowing, and manifesting itself in new ideas. Everyone just rolled with it, because his vision is unlimited and changing all the time," she remembers.

The prop master found creative ways to come up with all the different products she needed, on a very limited budget. As much as they could, she and her team tried to work with things that already existed, and then added their own customizing touches. They were able to avoid a lot of mold changes, for example, by adding their own labels to generic bottles in order to make "miraculous" spring water, lotion, and cleaner.

From hands that create miracles, to avenging angels and vampire slayers, Courtney Jackson's life these days really is out of this world.

The Perfect Marriage: Career Matches Made In Heaven

Chris Ubick, Property Master
Glory Days, Legally Blonde 2: Red, White & Blonde, Monkeybone, among others

As an artistically inclined teen, Chris Ubick had already set her sights on the movie business. Starting first in fashion advertising, and then taking a position at the studios in the art department, she enjoyed her work, but still longed for a better fit. Her answer came when she accepted the invitation of a friend, who suggested they work together on a project. Ubick was thrilled to discover that working with props gave her the sense of fulfillment she had been seeking.

"Property worked for me because I'm very detail-oriented, and it required me to be more particular, concentrated, and focused. I got to put my hands into more things, into bigger bits of smaller things. I liked being able to fine-tune individual pieces and make them exactly right, instead of creating an entire environment," explains the property master.

Having picked up important tips from those who have gone before her, she remembers her predecessors, saying, "I'm really lucky to have worked with three of the best prop masters in the business."

Remembering her work on the surreal film *Monkey Bone*, Ubick says, "*Monkey Bone* is interesting because it's like two movies in one."

"The beginning of the film takes place in a normal state of reality. And then it goes into an alternate, surreal reality. So we had to push the boundaries of creativity, in coming up with things that were as fun and kooky as possible."

The story involves a lot of mythological creatures and accompanying props. Some of those creatures are placed in a modern day setting, so props had to be designed that were appropriate for that juxtaposition.

The originality and imagination that went into the creation of the props was rewarded. "We made dolls, punching bags, and an entire line of merchandise for sale," points out Ubick.

Appreciating a line of work which affords her the freedom to "take a month off and travel to Fiji or the French Polynesian Islands," the Los Angeles native thinks back to *George of the Jungle*.

"We shot in Hawaii for two weeks, and it was fantastic. Amazingly, it only rained on our days off."

Such lucky breaks in the weather came not from a special effects crew, but directly from the forces of providence. Such forces always seem to smile on Hollywood – and on Chris Ubick, who grew up in the land where dreams come true, imagining the day when she would somehow play her part in moviemaking.

Kelly Berry
Assistant Set Decorator/Buyer: **Garfield, The Italian Job**
Set Dresser: **Psycho** (remake),
(among others)

Kelly Berry is certainly a long way from her small hometown of Canton, Missouri where her dad was active in local and regional theater.

"I was aware of the world of film, but didn't know how to get there, or how I'd ever fit into it. I've got to say, there's a certain sense of destiny in finally getting here."

Berry was living in France, through the Cleveland Institute of Art's foreign study program, when she decided to head west for the film business.

"I was anxious to start my career, but for the first three or four years in L.A.," she recalls, "I knew absolutely no one in the film industry. In fact, I didn't even know what the job descriptions meant."

She tried her hand as a gallery director, painter, sculptor, and photographer. Then, finally, through being a still photographer's stylist, she got her foot in the door as an art department coordinator. After receiving her Masters in Production Design from the American Film Institute, Berry decorated for several commercials, and worked as a buyer on such films as *Batman*, the *Psycho* remake, and Robert Zemeckis' *Castaway*.

Alfonso Arau's *Picking Up The Pieces* was the long-time artist's first feature film as a Set Decorator.

"What appeals to me most about set decorating is creating the external definition of characters through their environment. Each part of a set is an opportunity for me to specifically map the psychology and actions of the characters. I still feel that it's art, but the canvas has gotten much larger."

Gary D'Amico, Special Effects Coordinator
Adaptation, Vanilla Sky, "**Providence,**" among others

Speical Effects Coordinator Gary D'Amico initially set out in pursuit of work on the other side of the lens.

"I wanted to be a still photographer, and seminared my way through UCLA Extension," he remembers.

While continuing his UCLA classes, D'Amico was brought on as a laborer by Universal Studios, and went on to work as a propmaker.

He explains, "The turning point for me came while I was taking photography and working as a propmaker, and I started seeing other aspects of the business I wanted to participate in."

It's easy for Special Effects Coordinator Gary D'Amico to see how much his photography background has come in handy.

"I can look at a mat box and know what lens they're using, and whether or not my steam is in focus. And from a photographer's standpoint, I know how the elements I'm setting in front of the camera are going to play."

In an interesting plot twist, his segue from propmaker to special effects man can be attributed to his ability to rebuild Volkswagen engines.

"I was working in the prop shop," he recalls, "and they suggested I go see someone in the special effects shop because they were looking for guys who could work on VWs for *Herbie Goes Bananas*. And they knew I'd rebuilt the engine in my Bug."

Lucky for the versatile craftsman, Disney happened to be "doing one big show after another," so in addition to *Herbie*, he racked up credits on *The Last Flight of Noah's Ark, Something Wicked This Way Comes*, and *Tron*. But it was going on location for *Baby, Secret of the Lost Legend* that cemented D'Amico's place in the special effects life.

"Going to Africa cinched it for me because I realized I was making a pretty good living doing special effects."

Having the ability to rebuild the engine on his Volkswagen might seem like a strange way to get into the special effects shop, but no stranger than the concept of having a good-looking bicycle land him a role in the David Lynch pic, *The Straight Story*. The coordinator got his SAG card by saying, "On your left, thank you," while bicycling past Alvin Straight, an eccentric character who sets out from Iowa on a three-hundred-mile ride aboard a lawnmower tractor. In addition to his bit acting part, which came about because David Lynch liked the looks of the special effects coordinator's bike, D'Amico was fulfilling his usual role on that film, as well.

"Alvin Straight's brakes fail coming down a hill so we had to rig that. Then, as his brakes fail, the fourteen-foot trailer he's got hitched to the back has to fishtail out of control. And as he's heading downhill, he passes a house on fire," D'Amico deadpans.

In addition to *The Straight Story*, D'Amico also worked on the Lynch film *Mulholland Drive*.

Reflecting on his work on TV's "Providence," the gifted father of two who lives in La Tuna Canyon, California notes, "The effects on this show may be subtle. I may be asked to do something as simple as a spritz on a window, or a steam effect that helps paint a picture with a fine brush. And then, on occasion, I get to blow up a car, or simulate a World War I battle sequence, and that breaks the monotony."

Wendy Ozols-Barnes, Set Decorator
The Missing, "The Division," "Providence," among others

"I've lived many lives," notes Ozols-Barnes, "like, as a young child, traveling all over the country with my mother. And I feel the many hats you've already worn, and your life experience, are things you bring to this craft. If I'm doing research on a film, I can go watch other movies to pick things up, but it's not the same as actually having lived in a trailer, and being intimately familiar with how the little rose garden might look through the window. It's that layer – the life layer – that adds to your capabilities and your feeling of accomplishment."

Wendy Ozols-Barnes realizes that her rich background is an asset she carries with her to the set every day. The "Providence" Set Decorator was born with an artistic eye, and grew up around the collection of colors, symbols, and images that eventually became known as "Santa Fe style." It was after extensively traveling the country, and living in a van with her mother, that they eventually settled in Taos, New Mexico, with "a colorful collection of people."

Demonstrating her orientation toward detail, she continues, "People don't realize that Santa Fe style was developed by the old hippies that used things that were available to them cheaply, and ended up creating a style. They would go into the Andes, and bring back serapes to throw over an old sofa." And then she adds, smiling, "but I never saw a purple coyote. Where did purple, howling coyotes come from in Santa Fe style?"

Seeking a fuller expression of herself than her life in a small town allowed for, she came to live near a friend in Los Angeles. After a couple of detours, her creative sensibility led her to the movie industry.

Prior to becoming a decorator, the well-traveled Ozols-Barnes was the Lead Person on *Bad Girls*, a western on which "Providence" Art Director Chip Radaelli also served. She reports a "great fondness" for the genre, and says that coming from New Mexico, "westerns are kind of in the blood." She points out that the Victorian color palette she used on that western would surprise most people.

"True Victorian colors are a lot brighter than most people realize. What people tend to think of as Victorian has actually been weathered for a hundred years. The real colors they used were a heck of a lot brighter."

She also worked on the mini-series *Mr. Murder*, under Set Decorator, Michael Taylor, with whom she says she was fortunate enough to work on several occasions.

"It was interesting because it was medical science fiction," she says, "which required a lot of research. And because we had to dress a hundred and ten sets in forty days. When we actually pulled it off, I figured if I could do that, I could do anything."

"Providence" was Ozols-Barnes' first network series, but as

a decorator, she also has to her credit a Hallmark Hall of Fame mini-series, *The Ransom of Red Chief*, and an HBO film, *The Cherokee Kid*.

Referring to "Providence," she reported that working with Producer Mike Fresco and a "fantastic group of people" made it easy for her. Not to mention the fact that the production designer was her husband, Guy Barnes – which meant that they could "discuss things at home instead of having to schedule a meeting."

The decorator notes reflectively, "You don't always see what we do. In fact, people probably see half of what we do, at best. But," she goes on to explain, "even if it's just a basket of fruit, and I can make sure it's done really well and smells great, and the crew comes on set and it makes them feel good, then the chances of our work getting into the shot are really good."

The artist reported, "I really enjoyed myself on 'Providence,' despite the fact that some days were hard, and sometimes I had to deal with politics, which can put a damper on things."

One of the reasons Ozols-Barnes was so much at home on that show was her wonderful crew. "They really were one of the most amazing crews. They were always right there to help," she raves.

Weaving together the many threads that make her who she is, she expresses an interest in spinning and dying wool at some point in time, and then reflects on her career.

"Every project is different and I'm really proud of what I do."

Michele Poulik, Set Decorator
"Huff," "The Shield," *Army of Darkness,* among others

Emmy Award Nominations:
1998, Nominated (shared), Outstanding Art Direction for a Miniseries or Movie, **"From the Earth to the Moon"**

Michele Poulik says that when she was a child, exploring the Mies van der Rohe architectural wonderland in which she was raised, she used to observe the everyday world, and then translate it into an environment designed to capture the imaginations of the neighborhood kids.

Poulik remembers, "We used to crawl around the bush gardens in the complex where we lived, playing in wonderful shrubbery caves. I made furniture, and decorated those little caves, turning them into my family's house, Tarzan's house, or sometimes a war hospital complete with nurses and soldiers. Whatever would match the game of make-believe we were playing at the time."

"The Huntress" was the first contemporary, true Americana set since childhood for the set decorator, who has made a name for herself doing period pieces and highly stylized shows. As Michele Poulik explains, she and her crew were intertwining the pages of a suburban scrapbook with the grittier edges of a true crime magazine.

The slice-of-life show, about the death of true-life eclectic bounty hunter Ralph "Papa" Thorson, posed the most subtle of all challenges for a set decorating team, because sometimes the ordinary, rather than the obviously fantastical or extraordinary, can be the most tricky – and the most fun – to tackle.

As the story goes, Thorson nailed many slippery criminals, building a legend around himself that his death could not diminish. Unfortunately, infamy alone could not pay the bills when he was killed, and his wife and daughter were left trying to keep the wolf from the door. His death marks the beginning of the television series "The Huntress," and the start of the journey from housewife to bounty hunter for Dottie Thorson, who must step in and fill her husband's shoes

The episodes follow the triumphs, pratfalls, and foibles of Dottie Thorson and her daughter, as they learn to negotiate their way through the traditionally, steadfastly masculine landscape of bounty hunting for hire.

Slotted for a pilot and thirteen episodes, the crew was busy with the permanent sets, including a two-story San Fernando Valley house where Dottie Thorson has her office, the bail bondsman's office, and the jail.

It was not hard for Michele Poulik to relate to Dottie Thorson. After studying fine art, she accidentally discovered filmmaking, while attempting to fit the square peg of her artistic soul into the round hole of Corporate America. A fish out of water at General Motors, she was working on blueprints for car parts, when she decided she could create superior automotive manuals, if she was allowed to employ the use of videocameras.

So Poulik took a film class. And her life took a twist. Like a scene straight out of a spy flick, one day after class, she walked off with the identical handbag of a fellow classmate who was working on a film called *Thou Shalt Not Kill Except*. The switch led to a conversation, an invitation for Poulik to work on the film, and the eventual forming of their own production company, Sparkle Films.

Like Dottie Thorson, Poulik and her femme accomplice set out to prove they could excel in boys' town, and made their own short film, for which they won accolades on the film circuit. Poulik earned her industry stripes producing and art directing for commercials, as well as assistant decorating, working lead, and shopping for features shooting in Detroit. Eventually her work partner found a life partner and got married, so Poulik decided to follow the stardust out to Los Angeles, where the productions she had worked on had originated.

Poulik knew she had arrived when she was given the chance to work on *Army of Darkness* for Sam Rami, whom she knew from Detroit, and on John Woo's *Hard Target*. She still retains the innocent delight she felt as a little girl crawling around in the bushes, looking for found objects that could turn a cave into a home.

And she raves about the crew who helped her put the personality into "The Huntress," saying, "They backed me one hundred percent and worked so well with other departments, it's incredible. They made coming into work each day a real pleasure."

Eugene "Geno" Freiburger
Property Master: **"Just Shoot Me"**
Construction Laborer: *The Fabulous Baker Boys*
[worked on: **"Mad About You"**]
(among others)

"I thought I'd end up being a performer, until I had a professor in college tell me that unless it was an itch that I absolutely had to scratch, I should just forget about it," remembers Eugene "Geno" Freiburger.

The "Just Shoot Me" Property Master said that the combination of the variety, the number of people he had to please, and the responsibility of making everything functional on the show, satisfied his desire to perform.

"I got to do goofy, high-tech, tongue-in-cheek stuff, like the time I had to create a special briefcase with an electric handle. I love to sink my teeth in, and be right in the thick of things."

Originally an I.A.T.S.E. Local 18 stage hand in Milwaukee, Freiburger did loading and unloading for theater and rock concerts.

"I had so much fun at the concerts, that my hearing is shot from talking to the bands offstage," he reports.

The property master also had a stint as floor manager for a Milwaukee news station. When he was ready for a change of scene from the small town, he took a computer job in Los Angeles at radio station KHJ. After a year or so, he longed to get back into the production end of the business.

Several twists and turns in the road later, he went into property. He worked on the episodic "Quantum Leap" and *The Fabulous Baker Boys* feature before "Just Shoot Me," which he calls "a once in a lifetime opportunity and the most comfortable thing I've ever done."

He remembers a less serene time.

"I used to work on commercials and it was incredibly intense. The amount of importance they put on whatever product I was working with, made it the most stressful thing I've ever done. I was compensated monetarily but I was taking it too seriously."

He reports that when he discovered episodic work – first on "Mad About You" and "The Nanny," and then on "Just Shoot Me" – the stress was gone. Instrumental in keeping things running smoothly on "Just Shoot Me" was his much appreciated assistant, Abby Rayve.

"It wouldn't have been possible without her on the front lines," he states.

The property master says that one of his priorities on the show was making sure that George Segal had cigars – and the banjo he plays in many episodes. He calls Segal "a crack-up, with one of the heartiest laughs I've ever heard." He also got a big kick out of David Spade, who is "the wryest, and the most fun."

He raved, "We're like one big family, from the producers

to the stars to the crew. A lot of people work in this business for forty years, and never get to experience something this special. If I didn't have to take a hiatus, I wouldn't."

Speaking of family, the seasoned professional shares a calming view of the ocean with his wife, Laurie, whom he married a few years ago at the same Wisconsin courthouse as five generations of Freiburger men before him.

Reflecting on his career, the prop master remembers one particular episode which called for him to create a children's book cover about a moose and a raccoon who are floating down a chocolate river in a canoe. It was like art imitating life for Geno Freiburger for whom, at work and at home, life these days is sweet.

The Perfect Marriage: Career Matches Made In Heaven

Bonnie Bennetts
Set Decorator: **"Just Shoot Me"**
Production Assistant: *Interceptor*
Lead Person: *Matilda*
(among others)

"While you may not see the bite marks on the pencil on television, it's still something I take time for and appreciate," says Bonnie Bennetts, Set Decorator for the popular sitcom, "Just Shoot Me."

Paying attention to detail is one of the keys to Bennetts' fulfillment.

"If you don't take pride in what the sets look like, smell like, and feel like, then it's not worth doing. I absolutely love what I do." And it shows.

The talented artist was on "Just Shoot Me" since its early days. The fact that it centers around a high-end Manhattan fashion magazine afforded her "the challenge of putting fashionable wardrobe out there, as well as high-end, interesting set dressing – all on a budget."

She says she learned the art of detail from Kathy Klopp and Anne Ahrens, with whom she worked on features, and Jennifer Polito "who gave me the chance to lead and to flourish. She's the reason I'm here today."

Bennetts worked lead for six years before "Just Shoot Me,"

her first show as a decorator.

After receiving her Fine Arts degree, she was pursuing a graduate degree in filmmaking, and spending her winters teaching skiing. As fate would have it, a PBS feature, *1000 Pieces of Gold*, which she describes as a Chinese western, was shooting nearby.

Bennetts recalls, "I'd just finished another gig ski instructing, and was home in Montana visiting my grandfather, who had seen an article about the shooting of the film. He handed me the phone number and said, 'Give them a call.' I tried to tell him those kinds of breaks didn't come that easily, that it was much more difficult, and first I needed to get my graduate degree. He said, 'Call anyway.' So I did, and I was shocked when they actually interviewed me, and hired me on as a crafts service person."

The experience afforded Bennetts the opportunity to get a bird's eye view of all the different crafts, and led to an invitation to work on a film that was shooting in Los Angeles.

"I worked all over the place – in craft services, as a second, second A.D. and even as a stand-in for Kathleen O'Hara, the actress. It was funny – I'd be doing my stand-in job in front of the camera, and someone would call me on my walkie-talkie asking for more water, or asking me to block off the street," she relates.

She had finally settled into the Art Department when "Dream On" with Wendie Malick of "Just Shoot Me" went union.

Now Bennetts is in charge of her own "terrific" crew, including Lead Person Tim Park.

"He's very helpful and he has a really great attitude. My swing guys, Freddy Waff, Toby Bays and Roger Knight, are also incredible."

Because of the variety of hats she has worn, the set decorator brings to the set the unusual pairing of a fine arts education with the experience of "knowing what it's like to be moving fridges and couches off a truck."

"It might sound like a strange combo to find in a boss," she admits, "to be obsessing about the color of a chair and also able to empathize with my crew – but it's great for all of us and we get along really well."

Michael Belgrave
Set Dresser: *Jane Austen's Mafia*
[worked on: **"The Huntress,"** *Gone in Sixty Seconds*]
(among others)

Working on the female action drama, "The Huntress," was a perfect fit for Gang Boss Michael Belgrave, who grew up in a matriarchal society punctuated with strong and supportive women. He felt right at home.

"In my life, the people I admired were always women, like my grandmother, for example. When I woke up in the morning, I had to look no further than the dining room table to find my hero," he relates.

He was perfectly at home in scenes where a woman is cast in a role typically held by an alpha male. For "The Huntress," the gang boss drew on his own childhood surrounded by the fairer sex, with tasks like undressing an office that was clearly designed for a man, and slowly accessorizing it "until you can almost smell the fragrance of the lady in charge."

"Whether it's O'Toole's house or her office," he said, "we were trying to be true to the domestic suburban spirit of the character, while tracking her journey into the mine fields of the private boys' clubs."

From the female-based "The Huntress" and *Miriam Title-baum, Homocide,* to the tougher *Jane Austen's Mafia* and *Gone in*

Sixty Seconds, Belgrave is ambidextrous – equally at home with women and the man's world in which they find themselves.

Gina August, Camera Truck Driver
Never Been Kissed, Star Trek 9, "V.I.P."

"I was driving a bulldozer and I loved it – it was like a big Tonka toy," raves Gina August, Camera Truck Driver on "V.I.P.," and one member of the large faction of females comprising sixty percent of the crew.

"This is a male-dominated business, and has been for years, so the women don't always get the opportunity to show what they can really do. But on this show, we get to do things we wouldn't normally get to do on other shows. We have the chance to drive every truck, and do whatever is called for."

After majoring in art in school, August began oil painting until she happened to find herself "in the right place at the right time," visiting a friend on the Warner Brothers (then TBS) lot. The dispatchers, having seen her around quite a bit from her visits, were "literally pulling people off the street" and asked her if she wanted a job.

The driver, who has worked on *Star Trek 9* and *Never Been Kissed,* enjoys going on location, and the variety her job affords her.

"It is an unusual job and I like unusual – the places you get to film, the people you get to meet – and it's all a great learning experience."

3

Rush Hour
The Long Hours and Demanding Schedules Behind the Glamour

Sure, working in the studios is magical, fulfilling and rewarding – but it's also extremely hard work.

For these specialists, there is no such thing as a monotonous, ordinary, nine-to-five work day. That's the good news. And, on a work-'til-you-drop, eighteen-hour day, it's also the bad news.

Between budget demands, time constraints, and the myriad of technical and artistic challenges, every day is a new adventure, lived at breakneck speed. This chapter gives you a feel for the sometimes hectic pace of working on a movie set.

Jeff Verdick, Transportation Co-Captain
Holes, Twister, **"Dark Shadows,"** among others

Not long after the night owls have finally crawled into bed, Transportation Captain Jeff Verdick is putting on his work boots, and making mental notes of what the day has in store for him. Rising between 3:00 and 4:00 in the morning, it is going to be a very long day.

"In transportation, we cater to every other department in this industry, because they depend upon us to get them what they need," Verdick reflects. "Our job is to effectively organize everything for everyone involved on a show, so their jobs will run smoothly."

Driving to the studio in the dark, he's usually looking at a fourteen-to-eighteen-hour stretch before he can clock out. And by that time, it's often so close to his call time for the following morning, that going home doesn't even make sense. So he sleeps in a hotel room for a handful of hours, before starting the cycle again.

Jeff Verdick explains, "The hours are horrendous, but you condition yourself, and after so many years, you get used to operating on three or four hours sleep. When the weekend comes, you do a lot of sleeping."

While the benefits and financial rewards are great, he admits that his schedule is hard on family life. Even when he wasn't on location, the hours routinely kept him from birthday parties and school plays, as his children were growing up.

Verdick was the transportation captain on "Brutally Normal" and worked on *Level 9*, a Paramount pilot about Internet terrorism. He also captained a CBS pilot called *Russo,* which was written, produced, and directed by the team responsible for the critically acclaimed HBO show, "The Sopranos."

One of his most memorable experiences was working on *The Postman,* shot in Arizona, Oregon, and Washington, when they had to fly cars in via helicopter over the mountaintops. Starring Kevin Costner, the film was set in post-World War III era, where all the conveniences of modern day life – like fossil fuel and electricity – had ceased to exist.

The Southern California native's relationship to both film and vehicles goes way back, and is full of ups and downs. He was a reluctant child actor, and at nineteen years of age, joined the Stuntman's Association. In a motorcycle crash which was not the result of a stunt, he crushed three disks in his lower back. He then decided that stunt work wasn't for him.

He never thought he would end up in the Transportation Department, until he met his mentor, Transportation Coordinator Gene Klinesmith. The coordinator took young Verdick under his wing, and set him on the road to a career in studio transportation.

When we spoke, he was recently engaged to be married, and said he'd been given a second chance at a family life.

Asked why he has stuck with transportation all these years, he replies, "Despite the hardships, it's gratifying to satisfy the different departments on the lot, and to see the whole company running smoothly because your department is doing a good job."

Ryan Effner
Propmaker: *She's All That*
Swing Gang: *Never Too Young to Die*
Special Effects: ***Nightmare On Elm Street: The Dream Child***
(among others)

During production of *Dude, Where's My Car*, Ryan Effner remembers thinking, "I've never seen another film move this fast."

He recalls, "One day, there were tools and no lumber, and a week later, we had forty-three people working, and walls going up faster than you can imagine."

Watching the quickness and precision of his crew on the mile-a-minute *Dude*, Effner says he was reminded of the great skill possessed by his crew.

"It's unbelievable how incredibly fast our guys can build things on short notice. I can't imagine this caliber of work being done anywhere but Los Angeles. This level of talent is not easy to find. To walk on stage and see the amount of progress from one day to the next is staggering."

As an example of the pace at which the crew was running, Effner remembers that on a Tuesday, he brought on a location foreman and only three days later, they had to start filming the first location.

He explains, "It's all because of a budget crunch – budgets

and schedules are getting more and more compressed. The expectation of doing more with less keeps rising."

At one moment, Effner and his crew had five locations prepping simultaneously, and two others sets being built on stage. What's behind the trend of producers setting superhuman speed standards while shrinking budgets?

Effner explains, "Producers see a crew do something amazing and accomplish the impossible. They watch guys pull a rabbit out of their hat, and they instantly come to expect it – which raises the bar for everyone."

David Scott
Graphic Designer: *The Island*
Property Master: **"Alias," "Felicity"**
(among others)

Putting into perspective the diverse challenges of television and film, Property Master David Scott explains that when he does features, he may be afforded three months of preparation time, whereas in television, he's often required to do the same thing in six weeks, with one third of the budget.

"With most television shows," he points out, "you have one pass at it. If it's not right, you go with it the way it is or do something else real quick. You don't have the time to redesign and rebuild it again, no matter how much money is in the budget. You still have to pull off quality work you'll feel proud to put in front of the camera."

Working on Disney's made-for-television version of *Cinderella,* starring pop singer Brandy, Scott recalls, "It was all high end royalty, and the whole production was done in Gustav Klimt style, which meant Klimtian golds and colorful royal purples. We did the famous glass slippers and the famous carriage, which was very intricate. We took a stock carriage, and designed it to look like a pumpkin wrapped in garden vines. Part of the appeal of that show was all the beautiful people and colors."

The California native grew up in an Air Force family, moving extensively. After undergraduate work in Florida, he finished his schooling at California State University, Northridge, receiving a B.A. in Theatrical Set Design and Lighting.

"I'm doing what I went to college to do," he happily reports.

Property Master David Scott did commercials for twenty years, before branching off into features like *No Mercy* with Kim Basinger and Richard Gere. But he chose to focus on television so that he could stay in town, and be close to his wife and children. Fate cooperated and presented him with "Sliders" and "Murder She Wrote," allowing him to pursue his beloved craft, without spending too much time away from his family.

And for Scott, it's not the work itself that he's most proud of, but the fact that he has always been true to himself and his priorities in life.

"My family comes first," he muses thoughtfully. "You can't buy family and friends, but you can always get a job doing something."

Angelo M. Amodio, Set Dressing Dept.
Lead Man: *Rescue Me,* **"Baywatch"**
Lead Person: ***Daughter of the Streets***
(among others)

Lead Man Angelo Amodio reports that for the series "The Huntress," the primary challenges were not man against nature, but man against time.

"Our biggest concerns have been related to scheduling. We had to get the permanent sets done and ready for the first episode on very short notice."

Integral to "The Huntress" is the time period. The 1960s architecture tells of the reckless, rambling, carefree era in which the show was set. The wide open spaces of San Fernando Valley and Pasadena created the perfect, loosely woven backdrop for a story whose tension rests as much in what is absent, as it does in what is seen.

According to the lead man, more episodes than not were shot on location, sending the crew to jail one day and to a kiosk in the mall the next.

"My work is never boring," relates Amodio.

The would-be welder only accepted a set dressing position because he saw it as a way in the back door of the prop shop. Over time, set dressing for shows like Aaron Spelling's "Family," "Dynasty," and "The Colby's" showed the lead man that there are some detours in life that put you exactly where you belong.

Jim DePue, Transportation Coordinator
"Without a Trace," *A Boy Called Hate*, "V.I.P.," among others

Among the particular demands of episodic TV is the tight timetable.

When we spoke, Jim DePue laid out a typical schedule on "V.I.P.," his first show as Transportation Coordinator.

"We are always preparing for the next episode, so we have to scout and find vehicles. Then we have to paint, repair, and rig them, at the same time that we're shooting the episode we previously prepped. So, we're keeping that going, moving from location to location, dealing with effects, and paint, and autos breaking down. Then on top of all that, we're wrapping the work from the previous seven days."

According to DePue, the cable show, starring Pamela Anderson, "is about a group of bodyguards who are matched against the best villains in the world, and week after week, overcome."

"It's not easy to deliver such a big action show on such a tight budget," he pointed out.

Instrumental in helping DePue keep all those balls in the air was a predominantly female crew.

"In this male-driven industry, the women's talents often remain under-recognized and get overlooked, but we're averaging about sixty percent females on this crew. There are all sorts of pluses to working with so many women. Having almost all females to turn to, I've learned to recognize that in a lot of ways, they're more attentive to detail than the guys. They're also extremely dependable and a very integral, important part of the team. They solve many problems before they even become problems," he raves.

DePue noted, "It's not just me that makes this happen. This show is definitely loaded with professionals and good people."

The native Californian spent his early years in the San Fernando Valley, surrounded by vehicles in need of attention. He was often found in his father's engine rebuilding shop, and later enrolled in vocational school where he learned to weld. Just as welding was beginning to pique his interest, his vocational schooling was unceremoniously brought to an early end.

"Just before eleventh grade, my dad pulled me out of vocational school and put me back in high school, because he'd learned that I'd lied about my age," he remembers, laughing.

Looking for a way to pursue his love for welding, which was undiminished by the vocational school setback, and realizing he'd "always been an ocean-type person," the young DePue joined the Navy as an underwater welder.

After getting out of the service, he worked for Cleveland Wrecking as General Superintendent in Charge of Demolition Projects, until he crossed paths with an old friend from high school, who had become a Honeywagon driver. His friend gave him his first industry job, driving Honeywagon craft service vehicles.

He got his union card on *City Slickers 2*, working for Bobby Hunter, the coordinator on that film.

"Bobby took me under his wing, and showed me how to be a coordinator."

He went on to do "Time Cop," "Sliders" and various Universal projects as a driver, but cherishes above everything else his first experience as a coordinator on a feature, an opportunity granted him by Bobby Hunter and Steve Nickolaides.

The feature, *A Boy Called Hate,* is remembered by DePue as both "the toughest, and most rewarding, project." The film involved a lot of "fantastic, low budget things, like moving Condors around in the sand, and cars catching on fire" in the Palmdale desert.

On "V.I.P.," there was a great sense of accomplishment for DePue in taking old automobiles and "turning them into classic Jay Leno cars." The transportation coordinator is especially proud of Priscilla, one of the old T-Birds he and his crew transformed from a junker into a classic.

"It almost became a character, because it was one of the main prop points of the show," he says. "It was a very difficult coup to pull off, in addition to the everyday miracle of just moving this company and keeping it going."

Home based in Calabasas, California, with his wife, Lottie, and his two kids, the craftsman who took a junkyard clunker and turned it into Priscilla ponders his life.

"In this line of work, there are no awards. But you take pride in what you do. For me, the most rewarding thing is to look back and know I made something happen, and that I've gotten to work with a lot of great people, and helped to keep them employed."

Daniel Turk, Construction Coordinator
Dancing at the Harvest Moon, Dude - Where's My Car?, Nurse Betty,
among others

In the midst of breakneck schedules and budget concerns, Construction Coordinator Dan Turk always tries to remember what is truly important in life.

"Trying to be happy, being honest, working together to create high quality work that looks good — these are the things that matter," reflects the coordinator.

If ever there was a movie that could challenge Turk's Zen philosophy, it was *Dude, Where's My Car*, a film which will go down in history for its rushed time lines.

According to Turk, "Everything on that production happened so quickly, it was quite a challenge to get all our ducks in a row. We had such minimal prep time, we really had to hit the ground running."

The coordinator and his crew were given only one week of building preparation, to start a thirty-six-day shooting schedule that ran six days a week. On the busy agenda were two interior sets, one for the San Fernando Valley residences of the lead actors, and one for their girlfriends.

The crew was also working with a lot of shapes and colors, moving quickly to erect an arcade that would house video games and booths. One set, known by the moniker "the punishment room," had some especially interesting touches. Turk describes a heavy arched dungeon set with metal bars.

"There were large stones on this set, and we had numerous options," he explains. "We could have created the stones out of wood, and had the plasterers coat over them. But we opted to have the plasterer form them by hand, as he felt it would be more efficient and turn out to be more realistic looking. The results were very impressive, and we were really pleased with the outcome."

Thankfully, Turk reports, the extreme time constraints did not defeat him or his crew on that film.

"Luckily, I was working with a great crew, giving me their best work. Between all those guys, I must have had millions of years of experience working for me. They find a way to measure up and make things happen."

Dude was déjà vu after *The Shrink Is In*, where the circumstances were very similar — very little prep time, very little money and many anxious people. Again, the coordinator and his crew rose to the occasion.

"When all is said and done," Dan Turk concludes, "all that matters to me is being known as somebody who is honest and truly cares about this business. I just want to be seen for my capabilities. Money, budgets, schedules — they all come and go. In the end, all you're left with is yourself, your happiness, your reputation, and your friends."

4

Once Upon a Time in America
Work Begins With the Story

For studio technicians, beginning work means thinking about the story, and how you are going to translate it in a way that will work on screen. Before anyone can build, dress, or decorate a set; create effects, or even start thinking about props, there's the story to consider.

The story is the real director here, showing these craftspeople exactly what to do and where to go with their work.

Scott Ambrose, Property Master
"Huff," "Any Day Now," ***Life of the Party: The Pamela Harriman Story,***
among others

While Property Master Scott Ambrose remembers, "Growing up watching TV, I was intrigued by how it was all made," he still derives his enthusiasm and enjoyment from the stories themselves.

"I find the development of the characters fascinating. One of the girls on 'Any Day Now' wanted to get married and have children, and the other was a tomboy. As they grew up, their roles switched. The other great thing about this show was that every day, we learned something new about the civil rights movement. We really got a feel for what was going on at the time."

Helping Ambrose breathe life into "Any Day Now" was Ambrose's outstanding team, including Eric Dennis and Butch Kitchen.

"I have a fabulous crew, and they are great at keeping things organized. In props, that's half the battle, just making sure you know where everything is, and that it is readily available."

With two different time periods to contend with, the crew had their hands full. For the past, the final product was done in black and white, with certain objects being designed and manufactured in the exact colors that were going to be keyed on during post-production. The present-day scenes were done in color, and revolve around pieces specific to the lives of the two girls, now grown.

"For example," notes Ambrose, "one of the women is an aspiring writer, so we got to design her first book."

Ambrose is never far from the starry-eyed kid who grew up in Rochester, New York, enraptured by the wooden box with the antenna on top. His curiosity drove him to get a B.A. in Television and Film. Afterwards, the New Yorker came to Los Angeles where he cut his teeth on video, before checking out the different departments in the movie studios.

Ambrose jokes that he gravitated toward props "because they get to play with all the toys." When he found out they also get to work very closely with the directors, producers, writers, and actors, he says that clinched it for him, because he loves feeling like he's right in the thick of things.

The property master's love of a well-crafted tale not only keeps him interested, it gives his props believability, which helps the audience lose themselves in the TV.

Just like the young Scott Ambrose did so many years ago.

Garrett Lewis, Set Decorator
Panic Room, I Am Sam, Fun with Dick and Jane, among others

Academy Award Nominations:
1989, Nominated (shared), Best Art Direction – Set Decoration, ***Beaches***
1990, Nominated (shared), Best Art Direction – Set Decoration, ***Glory***
1992, Nominated (shared), Best Art Direction – Set Decoration, ***Hook***
1993, Nominated (shared), Best Art Direction – Set Decoration, ***Dracula***

Emmy Award Nominations:
2000, Nominated (shared), Outstanding Art Direction for a Miniseries, Movie or a Special, ***Gepetto***

"*Gepetto* is a morality tale: we don't necessarily get exactly what we want. And even when we do, we don't recognize it," notes insightful Set Decorator, Garrett Lewis.

While working on the two-hour, made-for-television movie about Pinocchio and the toymaker who brings him to life, the Emmy and Oscar-nominated decorator thoughtfully reflected upon the timeless tale.

"When Gepetto first wishes he had a son, Pinocchio is transformed into a boy, and learns about life from Gepetto. But what Pinocchio learns is not what Gepetto set out to teach him," Lewis explains. "He was trying to teach him to learn from life experience, and Pinocchio misinterprets his teachings, filtering them through his own lenses, as we all do. When that happens, Gepetto's response is, 'This isn't the little boy I wish I had.' But in Gepetto's quest to locate Pinocchio after he runs away," the artist points out with a chuckle, "he discovers that perfect children are really rather boring."

According to Garrett Lewis, that project posed a myriad of unique challenges, because it takes place in fantasy villages of 1850s Italy. He and his crew were first called upon to breathe life into Villagio, the utilitarian town where Gepetto lives and pines for the son he never had. Then they created Idyllia, the perfect little town that Gepetto visits when searching for Pinocchio.

"The perfect place is easier to do because everything matches," notes the decorator, "but Villagio, the little village that represents all of our lives, is also quite lovely. Most people live in a quite contented way in their own environment. What's interesting for me is to figure out how to say that to an audience."

"We all have different interpretations of what's beautiful and what isn't. To do something obviously beautiful is one thing, but to do something uncomplicated and simple is a different challenge," explains the decorating legend. "Even within the framework of an agreed-upon 'perfect' Idyllia image, there's always another vision."

They started out with a "very concise European palette" of warm umbers, terra cottas, greens, ochres, and ultimately, in order to accommodate everyone's vision, added "pinpoints of primary colors."

The decorator believes there's always a way to feel good about jointly conceived artistic decisions, and a way to make them work without sacrificing his vision. And he never loses his team spirit, either.

Lewis says that his crew is indispensable, all of them are such a big part of making it work, and they always have a handle on the necessary subtleties. He says it's a terrific creative team and a great collaboration.

"Each film presents the challenge of creating the world in which it revolves," Lewis concludes. "And I love every bit of it. It's really been a joy ride."

Maybe the great spiritual masters were right — maybe everything we see in our outer world is just an outpicturing of that which is first born in our mind's eye.

Robert Cardenas, Jr., Property Master
Saved by the Bell: Wedding in Las Vegas
[worked on: "**Married with Children**," "**In Living Color**"]
(among others)

"While the Pilgrims on 'Thanks' attack life from the 1621 viewpoint, they're still the same issues we deal with today," notes Property Master Robert Cardenas. "Like the fact that parents don't have enough time for each other, because they have a household full of kids. Or the problem of addiction, which comes up in one episode as the entire colony gets hooked on tobacco."

When Robert Cardenas was growing up, dreaming of becoming a police officer, an armed robbery among a village of pilgrims on "Thanks" was not exactly the kind of crime scene he had in mind. And when he pictured a gun on his hip, he wasn't envisioning the lightweight custom wooden musket which he had to have manufactured for that same episode of "Thanks."

"In Living Color" and "Married With Children," two other projects on Cardenas's resume, also tackled controversial issues head on. As it turned out, Cardenas's own desire to be married with children pre-empted a career in law enforcement. And though it isn't the role he thought he would be playing in life, Cardenas thoroughly enjoys his work.

On "Thanks," the thirty-minute sitcom which starred Cloris Leachman, Cardenas got to work with producers Phoef Sutton and Mark Legan. Their dedication to authenticity afforded him the fulfillment of truly capturing the time period. With occasional exceptions made for comedic license, they took pains to be "accurate in the show's look, wardrobe and props" – which explains the blunderbuss musket.

As assistant property master on "Married With Children," Cardenas remembers one gag in particular. One episode called for a dead pigeon to fall at the feet of two actors – and for Cardenas, himself, to climb up into the grid and drop it from the beam.

"That was definitely one of my most memorable moments – having to drop a dead bird."

The world of sitcoms has been home to Cardenas since the beginning of his career, mostly because of the freedom it affords him to pursue his family lifestyle, including participating in soccer, both as a player and as a certified USSF soccer referee. Weekly television also grants him plenty of opportunities to laugh, and the means to express himself artistically.

"I enjoy the schedule of working up to a performance – taking a week to get everything up and running," the talented worker relates.

With performance in his blood, it's no surprise to hear that Cardenas dabbled in both acting and music. "I was aware that whatever I ended up doing for a living, the desire to perform would have to find expression. Working in props satisfies that need in me because, just like the actors do, we are working right up until showtime. And then we get to perform."

Not one to play solo, the craftsman is grateful for his enthusiastic, skilled and reliable crew.

"I'm not a tennis player," he reflects. "I like being part of a team that comes together for a common goal."

Karen O'Hara, Set Decorator
Spider-Man, What Lies Beneath, The Silence of the Lambs,
among others

Academy Award Nominations:
1987, Nominated (shared), Best Art Direction – Set Decoration,
The Color of Money

Emmy Award Nominations:
1993, Nominated (shared), Outstanding Individual Achievement in Art Direction for a Miniseries or Special, ***Barbarians at the Gate***

"What fascinates me is seeing what people surround themselves with – how they invent themselves in the way they create their environments," says Karen O'Hara, set decorator on *What Lies Beneath.*

Reflecting the characters' personalities and inclinations through their physical environment was especially significant on this particular project, a thriller which revolves around their domestic life. The combination of the ambience and the location of the house – on Lake Champlain – was key in evoking the sense of the life shared by the couple portrayed by Michelle Pfeiffer and Harrison Ford.

"We tried to create a dream house that would reflect the special life this man and woman had made for themselves," reflects O'Hara.

Much of the film takes place in the house, which is really

a set of identical twin houses – one built in Vermont, and one on stage at Sony Studios. Karen O'Hara had also decorated twin homes on *Beloved*.

"It was challenging, trying to find two of everything – one for each house. And what we couldn't find, we had to manufacture," notes O'Hara,

In contrast to the couple with the right-from-the-pages-of-a-magazine life, their daughter plays in a grunge band. For that scene, O'Hara and her team created an eerily accurate replica of Al's Bar, a well-known, seedy music venue in downtown Los Angeles – complete with authentic graffiti and stickers on the wall.

"I have a very talented crew, with a good sense of humor, and I could never have done any of this without them. The construction and property departments were also amazing. This is a very collaborative medium, and that's been especially true on this film," noted O'Hara.

Working as part of an ensemble suits the set decorator.

She says, "At this point down the road, I choose projects based primarily on the people I'll be working with, rather than the film. The process is very important to me. I've been very fortunate to be able to work with a really wonderful group of people. We have a very good relationship."

Her relationship with her children also guides her choices these days – steering her toward productions that are based in town.

As a child, O'Hara was "always interested in painting, drawing, and making things." The set decorator, who blew in to Los Angeles from the Windy City, may have inherited her artistic sensibilities from her father, a fine art painter often found sketching at home.

Attending the University of Illinois for a degree in communications design, the artist worked for awhile in Chicago, and then realized she would have to choose between the East and West coasts if she wanted a career in art. Drawn to films, she dabbled in other departments before discovering that she liked to create atmosphere.

O'Hara's fulfillment comes from observing human nature, and then infusing her sets with the nuances she finds in real life characters. "I'm not tied to a computer or drawing board, so I'm out and about, interacting with other artists and craftspeople, and seeing how people live."

All of which translates to a movie-going experience with richness and texture – which makes both her and the audience happy.

Laurie Dalton, Property Master
"That '80s Show," "Providence," "My So-Called Life," among others

Before Laurie Dalton ever sets out in search of the props she needs, she takes a journey inside the story. For it's there that she can step into the shoes – and the state of mind – of the characters. For the property master who had been raised in Orange County, California, the interesting challenge while working on "Beverly Hills 90210" was "To put myself in the shoes of a teenager, to find what's hip and young and beautiful to these kids in Beverly Hills."

Again, on "My So-Called Life," which Dalton called a favorite, wonderful experience with real quality writing, she had to enter into the mindset of a teenager.

As she put it, "This time, I was a teenager from the Midwest who didn't have a lot of money, and was going through very real predicaments, rather than a teen acting out fantasies in fast cars. I would ask myself, 'If I was that kid, what would I take to school? What would be special to me?'"

By the time Dalton began her first season on "Providence," she felt like she was working in a bubble, because the shows were being made but not aired. Finally, about ten episodes into the season, they were brought in as a mid-season replacement and started getting some feedback – and at first, it wasn't encouraging.

"The initial reaction was negative – everyone, including the critics, hated it," Dalton points out. "We were getting ready to be cancelled, when it suddenly turned around. The public loved the show, and I think one of the main reasons is that the writing really touches people."

Although the show got off to a slow start in the ratings, when we talked to Dalton, she was looking forward to a nice long run.

"Providence" is a departure from the one-time high school teacher's usual fare of teenage angst. She said, "I'm lucky because I'm working on a family show again, but it's a nice change because this time it's young adults. There are no teens in it."

"Providence" was created by John Masius and was produced by Mike Fresco and Monica Wyatt, with whom Dalton worked on "My So-Called Life."

"Our producers are just delightful," raved Dalton. "They really bring a lot to the party, and I feel like I'm on a great team. Every aspect of this show is important to them – they live the show. The music, the props, the clothing – they don't overlook anything. And," Dalton added with a laugh, "that really makes you do a better job. It's like having a great schoolteacher. I'd much rather work for somebody who demands a lot of you."

Sydney Hanson, the main character, has a very active dream life, and Dalton reported reveling in the fantasy sequences that were a weekly part of the show.

"One week her mother comes back to life and they explore

all kinds of feelings together. Then another week, she's Cinderella or a World War I army nurse."

For the World War I army sequence, they went to Universal's European street, and Dalton's task was to come up with period medical supplies, stretchers, ambulances, and weapons.

For every real life story, we all have imaginary ones, as well, and for Laurie Dalton on "Providence," that's half the fun.

"All those fantasies are really challenging."

5
Mission Impossible
Tricks of the Trade

When it comes to working in movies and television, there's no such thing as impossible. Some challenges are just more challenging than others.

Every day, studio workers pull off the impossible so that every time we turn on the TV or go to the movies, we can see something incredible – and believe what we're seeing.

Studio workers talk about those shows where they have to call on everything they have, and everyone they depend upon, to rise to the occasion.

Charles "Charlie" Belardinelli

Special Effects Coordinator: *The Moguls, What Lies Beneath*
Special Effects Supervisor: *Dogma*
(among others)

Visual Effects Society Award Nominations:
2004, Won (shared), Outstanding Special Effects in Service to Visual Effects in a Televised Program, Music Video or Commercial, **"Carnivale"**

A boat piercing a truck windshield with people inside the cab, immersing an actress in a tub of water, and an exploding floor on *The House on Haunted Hill,* all illustrate the fact that Special Effects wizard Charlie Belardinelli has more than just his reputation at stake when he goes in to work each day.

According to Belardinelli, the exploding floor was "one of the most interesting gags," because it had to look like some sort of creature comes out from the walls, creeps along under the floor, and proceeds to chase the actors down a couple of hallways before it explodes.

"The timing had to be impeccable so as to avoid having the breakaways blow up under the feet of the stunt people and actors," he notes.

If life saving is inherent in the job of a special effects person these days, so is the challenge of working hand in hand with visual effects companies. On *The Mask,* for example, Belardinelli says that the timing and interface of the mechanical special effects and visual special effects were so seamless, mechanical gags they had done were actually credited later as visual effects in a show on the making of the film.

Summing up *What Lies Beneath* as "the most demanding show I've ever worked on," Belardinelli was aided by Tom Bellissimo, and a magnificent crew.

"Your crew can make or break you. I had five or six guys with me all the time, and they have performed beautifully. They were really wonderful and I'm so proud of them."

They certainly had plenty to do on *What Lies Beneath.*

"This show included almost every atmospheric effect, along with huge mechanical effects that take place under water," explains the effects wizard.

In one scene, a pickup truck is carrying a boat and trailer and, upon impact, the mast of the boat comes flying through the back windshield of the truck, missing the stunt person "by a hair." Getting the gag to unfold precisely each time was a matter of life and death for Belardinelli and his gang.

Another demanding gag that took weeks to accomplish centered around a bathroom scene, where different bathtubs were used in order to make it look as if Michelle Pfeiffer is in a tub with the water rising and lowering over her head.

Belardinelli, who joined forces with long-time partner Tom Bellissimo on *What Lies Beneath*, had been living in Boston, building scenery and doing general construction, before "love and glory" brought him out to California.

One day, he borrowed two hundred dollars, packed up his toolbox and a pair of roller skates, and said "California, here I come." It sounds like the opening line of a film, but for the New Jersey-born special effects man, it was the beginning of Chapter Two of his life.

"I started out inch by inch as a carpenter, and one thing led to another," he remembers.

After meeting Bellissimo on *Nightmare on Elm Street*, they realized that together, they could make some professional dreams come true.

"Tom is very good at some things and I'm very good at other things," he explains, "so we've been able to complement each other in that way. We're like a system of checks and balances for each other."

"Special effects are a great mystery to everyone," he adds. "They go to the movies and wonder, 'How do they do that?' That's what makes it so exciting. Sometimes it's mirrors and wire, and sometimes it's just plain clothespins."

David L. Scott
Graphic Designer: *The Island*
Property Master: **"Alias," "Felicity,"**
(among others)

"There's no Pinocchio aisle at the toy store, no 1860s Italian wooden toy aisle," jokes Property Master David Scott, referring to the challenges he faced while working on *Gepetto*, the made-for-television version of the classic tale of a wooden boy who comes to life.

"So," he continues, "every single thing had to be designed, keeping in mind the context and flavor of the show."

Scott goes on to explain that none of the toys on this film were mass-produced. Since each toy was so specific, everything had to first be designed and sketched out, and then fabricated in wood, or materials that looked like they were carved out of wood.

In the opening number, kids go running up to Gepetto's toy store, which has been closed all winter long, screaming excitedly for their favorite toys.

"We had to build flying fish toys that actually fly, dancing monkeys, climbing monkeys, and little toy soldiers that dance with the children," the property master remembers with pride.

The TV musical, produced by Jim Pentecost and Mike Karz, and directed by Tom Moore, is a new spin on the Pinocchio tale.

It stars Drew Carey as Gepetto, and Julia Louis-Dreyfuss as the Blue Fairy.

"Since *Gepetto* takes place in the 1800s, pre-industrial revolution, there were no high grade alloys or aluminum. They had only forged metals — brass, tin and steel," notes the property master. "Everything had to have that nice Old World flavor, but still have the incredible craftsmanship of the best toymaker in the land, which was Gepetto's legacy."

One of the most fulfilling tasks for David Scott was building the wooden period tricycle that Pinocchio rides down the cobblestone street. First, he had to build the whole bike out of metal, and then cover it with skin to make it look like wood. When he brought it to the set, everyone kept swearing it wasn't the same bike.

He just grinned and said, "I told you the next time you saw this bike, it would be wood!"

John Roth, Special Effects Technician
"The Division," *Guilty as Charged, Picking Up the Pieces*, among others

"We took steel, cement and termite-infested wood to make *Titanic* but it was all artistic license," explains Special Effects Technician John Roth, remembering work on the *Titanic* remake.

"In reality," he continues, "so much time had passed that the marine life would have eaten all the wood, and all you would have seen was a lot of unexciting metal, rusted smooth over the years."

Roth, who worked as right-hand man to Special Effects Coordinator Eddie Surkin on *Picking Up The Pieces*, demonstrated an innate talent for special effects, even as a young boy planning to become a rocket scientist.

He says, laughing, "I used to make rockets and use matches for fuel. Then one day somebody burst my bubble, by pointing out that the closest any of my rockets ever got into space was when they narrowly missed my head!"

Long ago having graduated from the days when he used matches for rocket fuel, Roth has nevertheless maintained his early ingenuity and imagination, and put them to good use on films like *Titanic*. He built the staterooms, which helped set the tone of the film in the opening sequence, when modern day crews are surveying the underwater wreckage.

Starting in television at Desilu, Roth left his mark on shows that would later be remembered as classics, like "Star Trek," "Mission Impossible," "Mannix," and "Family Affair." Those early experiences gave him a great foundation for this high-tech age, in which he's often required to pull a rabbit out of a hat – like when he looked at the magician's sketches he was supposed to follow to make the magic box, in which Sharon Stone is cut in half by Woody Allen for *Picking Up The Pieces*. The sketches called for forty-nine-inch-square pieces of a type of wood that only comes in forty-eight-inch pieces.

That same film was rich in Mexican tradition and celebration, much of which involved fireworks.

Roth reports, "For the El Torito tradition, they take a bull made of wire, and cover it with fireworks – like Roman candles. Then a guy has to get inside and run around terrorizing people. We ended up having to build it out of steel, with fireproof material covering everything but the head, which is foam with fireproofing. At one point, Woody Allen runs up to the bull while the fireworks are shooting out of it, so it was a real safety challenge for us."

At another point in the story, a wheelchair-bound villager played by Pepe Serna is transformed by the powers of the miraculous hand that's at the center of the tale.

"Since Serna is able-bodied, we had to build a false bottom into the wheelchair, for when he receives the miraculous cure and begins to grow legs."

The fact that Roth ever made it past the guard gate at Paramount was, in itself, a miracle.

"Paramount was close to home," he says, "so I stopped by and asked the guard if there were any jobs. Of course, I got turned away, but I didn't realize the guard wasn't in charge of personnel!"

Then he noticed there was another studio right across the street — Producer's Studios which later became Raleigh Studios — so he decided to try his luck there.

Roth recalls, "On that particular day, the studio was abandoned except for a lone guard. I remember asking him if they had any jobs for carpenter's helpers, and he told me, no, they didn't hire anyone at all there. But then the guard said, 'Hey, wait a minute,' and he pulled out that day's issue of *Variety*."

The guard showed him an article, talking about how the State of California was joining forces with I.A.T.S.E. (International Association of Theater and Stage Employees) to start an accredited apprenticeship program. And that, as they say, was that.

Special effects expert John Roth concludes, "Eddie Surkin and I, and a whole bunch of other guys, wouldn't be where we are today if it wasn't for the apprenticeship program. People coming in now don't have the wherewithal to get this vast knowledge from the old-timers by doing steady studio work. My teacher, Vic Delgado, is really one of my heroes, not to mention Ed Leroy and Milt Olson, God rest their souls. I really started in a golden time, and it's been very worthwhile."

Lauri Gaffin, Set Decorator
Zathura, Fargo, Lethal Weapon, among others

"That film was all about fear. The upstairs was supposed to be beautiful Art Deco, contrasted with a downstairs that was a chamber of horrors," recalls Set Decorator Lauri Gaffin, remembering the making of *House On Haunted Hill.*

The Joel Silver remake of the William Castle classic, originally starring Vincent Price, could have been a small budget nightmare for Gaffin, but luckily she doesn't scare easily – as she proved by returning to the business after a short detour. Buying old furniture and hospital items, and then picking up items at junkyards for *House On Haunted Hill,* she was able to get the raw materials she needed without going into the red. Then she and her crew added paint and flocking to age everything.

Gaffin explains, "We were trying to make everything look horrible and scary, and also get that 1930s period feel, while still working within a small budget."

Starring Geoffrey Rush and set in a sanitarium, the picture was filmed in Santa Clarita, California. "We created all these hallways and underground mazes with piping, and then we had to create depth, and a feeling of being underneath the ground," the decorator continues.

Gaffin says, "My crew makes my job so much more worthwhile and fun, because we work together so well and they're so much a part of everything I do. In fact, on *Fargo*, I even got to work with my father, who was hired as a driver. That is one of my favorite memories."

"I think it's really about a great story and interesting characters," the decorator notes. "You give me those and I can make anything look good."

John Villarino, Construction Coordinator and Past-President (for six years) of I.A.T.S.E. Local 44
Minority Report, What Lies Beneath, Jurassic Park, among others

If you look at the enormous bridge he and his crew built for *What Lies Beneath*, it's hard to believe that Construction Coordinator John Villarino was ever a novice, learning to make his first wall out of particle board and two-by-fours for the *Quincy, M.D.* pilot.

For *What Lies Beneath*, Villarino and his crew made a carbon copy of a bridge arching over Lake Champlain, between New York and Vermont, that measures three hundred seventy-eight feet in length and is thirty-five feet tall. "We built it on stage, and then moved it out to Playa Vista and put it up like an erector set," explains the coordinator.

With twin sets on *What Lies Beneath*, the coordinator needed to double his foremen as well. His long-time general foreman and brother, Mike Villarino, worked with him, as well as Co-General Foremen Denis Cordova and Rob Van Dyke.

"We built two houses that were exactly the same – one in Vermont and one here. We had to be technically correct, and careful to make sure the hardware, doors, and windows were exactly the same," states Villarino.

He raves, "My whole crew is fantastic. Most of the guys have been with me for years and years, and I've also found some great new people. I've got a great paint crew and laborers. It's nice to walk in and know your crew has everything under control, and they're going to make you look good."

Villarino remembers being the new kid on the block. Fresh out of the Navy, with no idea where his path might lead him, the New Yorker who had grown up in the Bronx happened to be in the right place at the right time "when Walt Hatfield needed some bodies at Universal." Villarino found out about the opening because Hatfield's wife happened to know someone at Dunn Edwards Paint, where Villarino had been working.

It didn't take long for the movie business to get into his blood. Strangely, every location Villarino found himself on was like déjà vu – they were all the places he had been stationed as a young man in the Navy. He reports feeling like history was repeating itself, "except," he jokes, "this time I had money."

"When people are watching a movie, they never see what goes on behind the action. It's much more interesting to look behind the set walls than in front of them," he muses.

Following his freshman efforts on "Quincy, M.D.," John Villarino systematically built his repertoire as he built more sophisticated sets – like the 747 aircraft constructed out of steel and fiberglass for *Airport,* and the huge bridge for *What Lies Beneath.* Over the years, as his skill and talent grew, productions also became larger in scope. Massive productions like *Jurassic*

Park, in which they had dinosaurs on stage and built all the hills and mountains, and *Waterworld,* where they found themselves working with one hundred tons of steel, became commonplace in the industry.

"To me, this life is like being a circus roustabout. You come to a stage, you build a set, then you leave. Just like being in the circus – you go to a town, put up the tent, invite everybody to come see the circus, and then you tear it all down and move on. We're like nomadic traveling gypsies. We're only on a show for a little while, whether it's one day or fifteen months. This is circus enough," he says with a smile.

Villarino concludes, "There's a certain aura or mystique that goes with this job – the magic of Hollywood. Tell someone you work at Jiffy Lube and they say, 'Oh, great,' but tell them you work in Hollywood, and they won't stop talking to you."

Lawrence "Larry" Needham, Special Effects Technician
[worked on: *Jaws 1, 2* and *4, The Chase,* **"Bewitched,"** among others]

"I'll never forget the day I missed an important doctor's appointment, because we were trying to capture a twenty-eight-foot boa constrictor that had gotten loose and wrapped itself around my leg," Larry Needham remembers with a laugh. "When I told the doctor why I'd missed the appointment, he said, 'That has to be true. No one could make it up.'"

Such strange encounters were all in a day's work for Needham. Like the time that he found himself in a railroad car, face to face with three live Brahma bulls on *The Chase* with Robert Redford.

Only half-joking, he says, "I'm lucky to be alive," and reports, "a missing part of a thumb, seventeen busted bones, a broken nose, a busted wrist, and more burns and scrapes than I can remember," in his thirty-plus years as a Special Effects man.

Thinking back on the snake, he says that he was filling in on "The Wackiest Ship in the Army" when they were shooting a scene where the crew of a PT boat was supposed to be walking along an island, come to a hill, notice the boa constrictor heading down the hill and stop, startled. There was an animal trainer who was hiding behind an artificial rock at the top of the hill, and when the cameras rolled he was supposed to let the snake out of a big sack, and the snake was supposed to crawl down the path.

According to Needham, the hill was made of plywood two-by-fours and covered with sand. So the snake starts down the hill, sees all the cameras, the lights, and fifty people, and decides to make a left turn.

"He crawled in between the two-by-fours," Needham recalls, "and he was gone. The director said, 'Hey, get that snake back so we can try that again,' and we said, 'Yeah, you mean when we find the snake!'"

He chuckles. "I'll never forget the look on the director's face as he said, 'You mean to tell me we've got a twenty-eight-foot snake loose on stage?' Needless to say, forty people left the stage. Quickly."

They finally found the snake and, between the animal trainer who finally got a hold of its head, Needham's co-worker, Ira Anderson, who took hold four or five feet behind him, and a grip who got a hold of the back part of the snake, Needham was left holding the tail. Thirteen feet of snake wrapped itself around his leg in a vise grip – and relieved himself on the special effects man, to boot. They eventually got the snake back into the sack by slowly unwinding it, leaving Needham with a sore leg, a missed doctor's appointment, and a moment he would never forget.

His long career is full of such unforgettable moments, and such impossible challenges. The son of a carpenter, he had a hammer in his hand from as far back as he could remember.

"I recall building things around the lake where we lived. There were a lot of tall trees around the lake, and we built a lot of tree houses. We would take planks and run them from one tree to the other, and have swings like Tarzan. You could travel a long way along the lake on those swings, twenty to thirty feet off the ground."

The New Englander's first job was working as a water boy – on skyscrapers. His father was building a bank in downtown Providence, and men would be out on steel girders welding and riveting. Needham would carry a bucket full of water in each hand "so I could balance on the six-inch steel beams," and he had a dipper in each bucket. He would walk up to the guys who were working, and offer them whichever bucket was the fullest.

Never one to be daunted by the impossible, a young Larry Needham decided at fourteen years of age that he was ready to be on his own. So he headed from Rhode Island to Southern California with little more in his pocket than a bus ticket that would get him halfway to where he was going.

"When I left home, I only had a vague plan. I didn't have enough money to get all the way to Los Angeles, so I went from the tip of New England to Florida. I always loved to fish, and thought maybe there was a fishing boat union I could join."

Hitchhiking and starving much of the way, he remembers walking, dazed and near dead from lack of food, all the way from where the bus let him off somewhere in L.A. to Arcadia, where he knew his uncle lived. It wasn't time for Hollywood yet, and the runaway ended up back in Rhode Island. Eventually, his family relocated to Southern California because the New England winters were hard on his father, who had lung trouble.

Needham, Sr. was working as a carpenter foreman on the building of CBS Television City in Los Angeles and one day, they needed maintenance men, so he and his son both went to work as studio maintenance men.

"I'll never forget," remembers Needham, "someone had taken the big CBS eyeball off the building to paint it or something and I was putting the eyeball back up there. I'm on a scaffolding with four-foot-tall letters, way up near the top of the building. It was around one or two in the afternoon, and all these guys in suits are coming back from lunch. I can see them down on the sidewalk, waving their arms at me and yelling something. Finally, someone comes up over the parapet wall on the roof to tell me I am spelling 'television' wrong."

Spelling may not be his strong suit, but television definitely was, from "Bewitched" to "The Iron Horse" and "Knight Rider." Working in maintenance construction, he watched the union guys in the set builders union, and noticed that their work looked a lot better – and steadier – than the outside construction he was used to. Eventually, he was laid off as a maintenance carpenter, and returned to outside construction, but the idea of working on the actual movies and television shows never left his mind.

Larry Needham must be part cat – for he survived more than his share of close calls. The snake didn't kill him. Walking across hundreds of planks and scaffolding never did him in. And he survived the close encounter with the Brahma bulls. He even got out alive after an incident on "The Iron Horse" where the wrong building was blown up.

"I almost got blown out of the side of the building!" he recalls.

Dale Robertson was supposed to ride in and blow up a small town. It was set up to where he was supposed to run into a building with dynamite in it, come out with the dynamite already lit, and throw it at these buildings, one after another. When he threw the dynamite at one of the buildings that held munitions, there was supposed to be a tremendous explosion from inside, blowing out the front of the building.

They had rehearsed it just before lunch, but someone made a misstep and blew up the building where Needham would have been standing. Thankfully, Needham had a premonition and changed the plan – just in the nick of time, so he wasn't inside.

He almost wasn't so lucky when he climbed under a car on "Knight Rider," undid the nuts and bolts expecting some light wood to fall on his face, and got hit with a ton of metal instead, breaking his nose.

"Someone punched holes in pieces of metal instead of wood without telling me," he explains. "So this avalanche of steel came down on me. It's the nature of the business. These things happen."

Being a special effects man is a challenge any day of the

week, but when you take them off the studio lot where they have everything at their fingertips, and send them on location, the difficulties are multiplied tenfold.

Needham points out that being on location, in "some of the strange places they decide to shoot," there are mosquitoes and other elements you're not used to dealing with – and often, none of the conveniences of home. He says that in his years of working on location, it wasn't unusual to run out of a certain kind of nut or bolt, or even a pack of cigarettes, and not be able to find it in remote locations.

Like in Antigua, when he couldn't get a chain saw to start, and he needed it "to cut down trees, and get the sticks and stuff we needed to build some native huts that pirates were supposed to live in." Where were they going to get a chain saw? They couldn't just run to the local Walmart or Home Depot, like they could in Hollywood.

"The thing about being on location," Needham points out, "it's not like it is when a tourist goes to an island or some other country. A tourist gets on a boat or a plane, goes to a hotel or a condo, and then located nearby – usually within walking distance – are all the things a tourist might want, like restaurants and things. On location, sure you may stay in a hotel, but the similarity ends there. You are in areas where people are not used to dealing with tourists – they aren't trained, they aren't prepared. And there's a terrible culture clash."

The New Englander cites as an example a shoot on *The*

Islands by *Jaws* writer, Peter Benchley. They had gone to an island that was "fifteen miles long and fifteen miles wide," where they processed sugar cane, and the natives lived a hand-to-mouth existence.

Needham and his fellow workers arrived before the shooting company, to do some scouting, to brainstorm on the rain scenes, and rig some pumps for pumping water. When lunch time rolled around, they asked the driver where they could get a bite to eat.

He told them there was a restaurant two miles down the road, so they went two miles but all they could see was a cinder block building. When they walked through the door, they were in a place that was maybe twenty-five by thirty feet, with only four or five tables.

"The menu was a little blackboard," Needham recalls, "and it said 'chicken, fish, and goat.' There were two pots. One had rice in it, and one had oil, so whatever you wanted went in the oil – the chicken, the fish, or the goat!"

Then there was a bunch of squabbling, and hand waving and gesturing, as the woman behind the counter tried to answer their questions about the menu.

"We wanted to know what they meant by chicken," he remembers, laughing. "After all, a fryer is usually a young rooster, and a roaster is an old hen. Was it fried chicken? Roast chicken?" Needham laughs.

"After the woman said she didn't know how old the chicken was, one guy said, 'Fine, I'll have the chicken.' The next guy wanted to know what they meant by a goat. Was it lamb or mutton?"

"After all," Needham says, still chuckling, "a lamb is a young sheep and a mutton is an old sheep."

"The woman said she didn't know how old the sheep was, and the guy said, 'Fine, I'll try the goat.'"

"Then the next fella started asking about the fish, and the woman waved her hands, exasperated, as if to say, I don't know if it's freshwater or saltwater fish, male or female, it's just a fish! It swims in the ocean! Fine, the guy said he would have the fish."

When Needham's turn finally came, he got straight to the point.

"I told her, I'll have the goat, but first I need to use the toilet. Where is it? So she points towards the door I came in. So I walk back outside, look around, turn right, go around the corner, go all the way around the building, and no toilet. When I come back in, she's still cooking. I ask her where the restroom is, and she points to the bushes!"

Then he asked, "Which bush?" And the woman told him, "Any bush you want."

When asked if they played practical jokes on each other at work, Needham replies, "Work played enough practical jokes on us."

Special Effects technician Larry Needham was always known as much for his sense of humor, as his ability to slip in and out of rubber sharks and other tight spaces.

Thinking about his life at the studios, he remembers the days when the football players from USC and UCLA would go to the movies for summer jobs. The late Glen Galvin, a special effects man whom Needham worked with, played football for one of the colleges – on the same team with John Wayne.

"The studios were supporting college football teams by giving these kids different jobs," the special effects veteran says, smiling. "One day, I looked at Galvin and said, 'You know what? You played football with John Wayne, Ward Bond and these other fellas, and then you came over here and worked in special effects with me. We all came over here on the same day, but they became big stars. We must've gone in the wrong door, 'cause we wound up special effects men instead of big stars.'"

He laughs, and says, "You come that close. John Wayne could've been a special effects man and I could've been a big star. In any case, my work was much more interesting than swinging a framing hammer," he reflects. "As the years went by, I was glad I was doing that kind of work. I never dreamed I'd be doing some of the things we did. It was mindboggling. Even though it was very time-consuming, difficult work, I realized I spent my life entertaining millions of people."

John Kersey, Construction Coordinator
"CSI: Miami," *Once in a Lifetime,* **"Providence,"** among others

"I like producers coming up to me and saying, 'I know this is impossible, but can you do it?'" says John Kersey, Construction Coordinator, who flourishes under the same pressure that makes many people wilt.

The coordinator talked about working on "Providence," the popular one-hour television series set in Providence, Rhode Island.

"A lot of times when you're working, you're just expected to build the sets, and the producers figure they'll get the look they want through decorating. But the 'Providence' producers definitely wanted clean, crisp sets, and they wanted it to look real, which is great for me. I love to make things look real."

Starring Mike Farrell from "M*A*S*H," the drama is the story of a woman who returns to her hometown for a funeral, and is convinced by a twist of fate that she should stay and once again make New England her home. Initially, the house that's the focal point of the show was shot on location in Providence, but was later built "totally from photographs" on Universal's back lot.

One of the craftsman's favorite memories from the first season comes from an early episode where they needed a boathouse, but couldn't afford to shoot on location at a lake.

"So, we rented a Doughboy pool, put it on a stage, and built a boathouse around it. We put algae and plastic on the bottom of the pool so it wouldn't look like a pool, and when we shot it, nobody could tell that the boat wasn't on an actual lake."

When the construction coordinator first read the script for "Providence," he admits that it seemed somewhat implausible to him. "I can't believe the way this group of actors was able to pull off the unbelievable, and really make it work."

Grateful for a "Providence" crew that has been with him for years, Kersey had a lot of confidence in them, and a soft spot in his heart for Keith Haugen, a laborer who passed away between the first and second seasons.

Before "Providence," it was "Moonlighting" that kept the challenge seeker on his toes. The California native has only fond memories of "Moonlighting," saying it was both "fun and hard work." The show was filled with last-minute opportunities to refine his craft, such as the time the script required Cybill [Shepard] and Bruce [Willis] to run up and down three stories of a stairwell — and at the last minute the location was lost.

"Around noon, the producer called and said we needed a three-story stairwell on stage by noon the following day. And the next day around 12:00 when the producer called, I still had a big crew working on it. He asked, 'Is it ready?' I said, 'No, but give me an hour.' And sure enough, when he called back at 1:00, we had the stairwell ready to go," remembers Kersey with pride.

Raised on eighty-five acres in Modesto, the California native spent much of his childhood milking cows on his father's ranch. Not surprisingly, young Kersey figured he'd grow up to be a farmer. Above and beyond being a rancher, however, his father was a general contractor, and it was from John Kersey, Sr. that Kersey picked up some of the basic tricks of the trade, working as an apprentice carpenter.

When he entered college to study forestry, Kersey took classes on an 8:00 a.m. to noon schedule, and he needed a job to fit around those hours. So, at first he was a very unhappy short order cook. Then he saw an ad in the paper that Universal Studios was hiring for construction work on the swing shift — which just happened to start at 2:00 p.m.. and end at 11:00 p.m. — the perfect hours to accommodate school. So the would-be farmer happily abandoned his chef's hat, and any thoughts of becoming a farmer.

Explaining what it is that keeps drawing him back to television, the coordinator who loves to prove that the impossible is possible, says, "Television is so much more sped up, so it's more of a challenge. When you get into features, it's a set thing. You come in a month and a half in advance and know exactly what you're going to build. But in TV, you don't know what you're going to build next week."

6

The Twilight Zone
Out Of The Ordinary

You've already heard about some of the mechanical, logistical, and safety challenges workers face. Now, you'll hear from those workers who have to leave the everyday world, and think outside the mundane.

Taking the ordinary and tipping it on its side takes a specialized perspective – not to mention incredible attention to detail and finely tuned skills. Whether it's blurring the lines between reality and surreality, jumping between black and white and color, or moving back and forth between the past and the present, it's a real balancing act.

As they used to say at the beginning of "The Twilight Zone" episodes, "You are about to enter another dimension…"

MONKEY BONE

Alternating between reality and surrealism, the film *Monkey Bone* takes its name from a comic strip drawn by the film's main character, played by Brendan Fraser. When fate steps in and alters the entire course of the animator's life, he enters a skewed version of his world.

Creating the film's twisted dream reality called for the ultimate in skill from the workers. Set Construction, for example, had the monumental task of building sets for every stop along the journey of imagination traveled by the hero. Among other challenges, they had to contend with forced-perspective sets that had to be constructed to accommodate Animatronics.

Special Effects, meanwhile, reported plenty of "Rube Goldberg"-type contraptions. Flying hot air balloons and bicycles, as well as intricate rigs, action props, and other sight gags, kept them busy. And thanks to the plethora of creatures in the feature, as well as the nightmarish tone of the piece, the Set Decoration department had plenty of opportunities to flex their creative muscle. They had fun capturing the mood and ambience of a carnival from an earlier era, reminiscent of the Santa Monica pier in days gone by.

And last but not least, the Property department had their work cut out for them, creating mythological creatures, cartoon dolls, punching bags, and an entire line of related merchandise.

Combining some of the most interesting and challenging techniques and technology in movie making today – including animation, live action, digital effects, and stop motion – *Monkey Bone* is a cinematic smorgasbord.

Jurassic Park I and II

The Color Purple

Lethal Weapon 2

Scrooged

Waterworld

Edward Scissorhands

Baby's Day Out

Toys

Beetlejuice

Joe vs The Volcano

Jaws

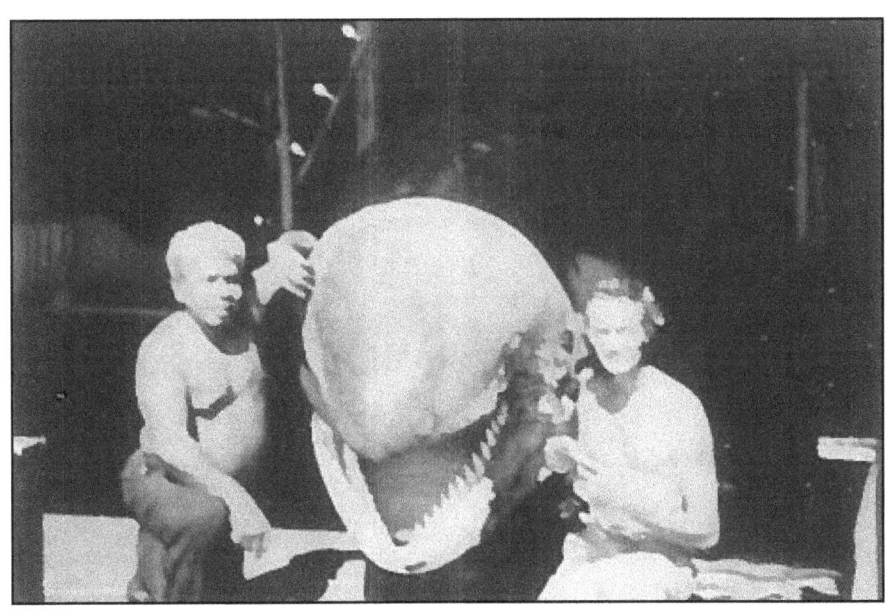

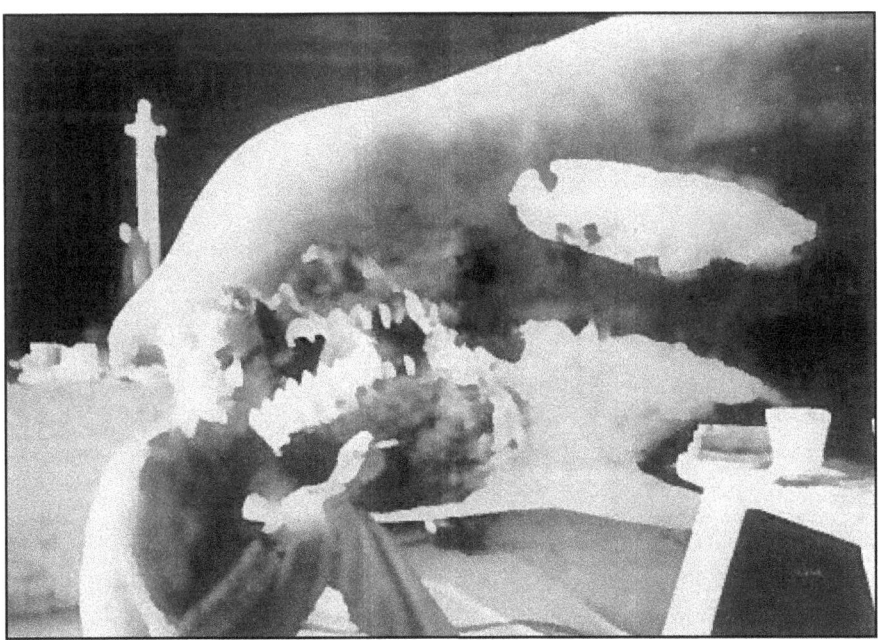

Jaws *photos from the collection of Larry Needham.*

Chuck Stewart
Special Effects Coordinator: *The General's Daughter, Con Air*
Special Effects Supervisor: *The X-Files*
(among others)

"*Monkey Bone* is mostly a sight gag show, with visual scenarios in nightmarish situations," explains Special Effects Technician Chuck Stewart. "It involved quite a bit of effects rigging, a fair amount of flying, and a lot of action props."

With about thirty crew members in full swing on the film, Stewart was delighted to report that "everyone was very self-reliant and self-motivated." All he had to do was give each one a task and then relax, knowing that they could think things through without his having to detail the work for them.

"Special Effects is one of the few 'learn by doing' jobs left," Stewart notes. "There is no school you can attend to learn this trade, other than the school of life where you pick the brains of those who preceded you."

The Ohio-born special effects man, who has lived in California since he was seven years old, was steered in the direction of the film industry by an elder family member. Growing up, he exhibited a great deal of artistic versatility. He enjoyed painting, drawing, and sculpture, and fully expected to have a fine arts career. After high school, he worked construction for a few years, and then "migrated towards property and special effects," thanks to his uncle, Dick Reseigne, a construction coordinator at the studios.

For Stewart, the common thread between the fine arts and special effects is the creativity and problem-solving aspect of each.

"A fine artist thinks about something he wants to create, then solves the problem of how to generate it and present it to the public. In special effects, we are essentially given an assignment, and the creative part for us is in figuring out how to solve the problems it contains."

While Stewart got films like *Con Air, The General's Daughter*, and *Logan's Run* under his belt before tackling *Monkey Bone*, he refers to *The Muppet Movie* as his turning point picture – a film that also blurred the line between reality and surreality, as the Muppets "came out of their world and into ours."

"We did a lot of innovative things," he continues, "taking puppeteers into the real world with blind drive cars, where a little person would drive from the trunk of an old Studebaker, so the puppeteers could sit in the cab and appear to be driving. We did the same thing with a bus and in fact, we created the largest Muppet ever made."

"Most people don't get to work with dynamic forces like we do," he notes.

A dynamic force to be reckoned with himself, Chuck Stewart is grateful for his line of work.

He asks, "How many people get to move tons of water, make hurricanes and tornadoes, or blow up buildings? These are the things the nine-to-five worker will never get to experience."

Paul Lombardi, Special Effects Coordinator
Bad Santa, The Last Samurai, Monkey Bone, among others

"On *Monkey Bone,* we got the chance to make things break that are supposed to be strong, and make things strong that are supposed to break," notes Paul Lombardi, who worked side by side with Chuck Stewart on the feature.

"Going against the current technology – that's what's fulfilling for me," he continues. "I love taking items and turning them around to our uses, or putting them to use in ways they're not normally designed for."

Speaking of an atypical twist on an old standard, one of the gags in the film was a flying bicycle with batwings – which is not exactly among Schwinn's usual inventory. Another airborne gag posed one of the Special Effects Team's biggest challenges. They had to create the illusion that a Macy's-size balloon had gotten loose and was taking the film's heroes on a wild ride across the countryside.

Lombardi explains, "We did it full scale, creating a mechanized system that was positioned over the top of the balloon, to animate it and allow the actors to bounce up and down. We took them over trees and put them into stunt traffic, where they were jumping over cars on cue."

The special effects technician modestly says these triumphs

are "nothing new, just another day at the races."

Perhaps the ability to take his work in stride was instilled in him by his father, who also worked in special effects.

Lombardi doesn't underestimate the power of stillness on the job, and says that the public would be surprised at how much special effects work is actually centered around idea sessions, which he calls "noodling." He explains that their work begins with initial conversations with the front office, figuring out what needs to be done, and is followed by returning to their shop to huddle and decide on a game plan.

Despite a body of films which depict external struggle, such as *Courage Under Fire, The General's Daughter, Siege,* and *Clear and Present Danger*, or the internal struggles central to *Monkey Bone*, the special effects technician who makes his home in the Northern California town of Los Altos approaches both work and life with a Zen tranquility.

Pondering the difference between the road less traveled, and the usual nine-to-five white collar life, he observes, "The main difference between what we do for a living, and the life of a guy who goes into an office every day, is the fact that every one of our jobs has a beginning, a middle, and an end."

He points out, "People don't realize that this is where movies are really made – here in the shop, brainstorming with each other. If it wasn't for the crew, we couldn't do the movie. It is definitely a collaboration."

"So many guys are worried about the digital effects and

optical people coming in and running us out of the business," he concludes. "Not only are they not going to hurt us, but they've actually created new challenges and opportunities for different ways of doing things. Believe me, when all is said and done, we're going to be around for a long time."

Jackie Carr, Set Decorator
"Las Vegas" (pilot), *E.T., Jurassic Park,* among others

"Movies with creatures in them seem to be following me," notes Jackie Carr, the set decorator who worked on *Arachnophobia, Gremlins* and *Jurassic Park*, and is often sought out for her experience with special effects-based films.

Attracted to the fact that *Monkey Bone* was rich with atmosphere, Carr said, "The fact that the set was like an old carnival on a pier was the main reason I wanted to do this project. As I was gathering all the old things, I could feel the creakiness, feel how decrepit it was, like the Santa Monica pier in ancient times."

The pier is the scene of a nightmare world which Brendan Fraser – an animator who draws a cartoon strip centered around a monkey – enters into when his life takes a drastic turn.

As for Carr, she thoroughly enjoys all the twists and turns her own path has taken, saying that every new show brings with it new adventures and opportunities. For *Arachnophobia*, for example, she was either flown in to work every day by helicopter or brought in by boat, as they were shooting at Angel Falls, the world's highest waterfall.

"I enjoy every show because there's always new subject matter, and I get to meet new people and travel to new places. And with special effects movies, the technology is changing so rapidly, there is always the excitement of coming up with new ways to work with cameras and effects. Every show is so different," she observes.

PICKING UP THE PIECES

Eddie Surkin
Special Effects Coordinator: **"The Division,"** *Picking Up the Pieces*
Special Effects Supervisor: **"Sliders"**
(among others)

It's not every day that Special Effects Coordinator Eddie Surkin has to hang an actor from a chandelier, string him with fireworks, and light him on fire. All this while protecting the safety of the villagers below, who are beating the actor like a piñata.

"That scene [in *Picking Up the Pieces*] was never even mentioned in the script," notes Surkin. "As soon as he saw the other firework combos I built, the director came up with the idea. He knew what he wanted but he didn't know how to get there, so I helped him."

On *Picking Up the Pieces*, Surkin worked with both Alfonso Arau, of *Like Water For Chocolate* fame, and Woody Allen.

"Arau is extremely meticulous and particular," reports Surkin. "And he likes to always take it to the edge of what you can do, in every sense of the word. We spent a lot of time together so I could give him what's available."

The eclectic comedy directed by Arau stars the unusual pairing of Woody Allen and Sharon Stone, playing lovers who join the witness protection program, and move from Brooklyn to the

Southwest in order to ditch Stone's mobster boyfriend. Through a series of dark comic circumstances, Stone's hand becomes a "holy grail," creating miracles for the entire New Mexican village where it turns up.

Woody Allen was a real trouper, a good sport, and a real professional, according to Surkin, who had stand-ins ready for the more difficult gags, but never had to use them.

Even for veteran special effects man Surkin, who has to his credit such films as *King Kong* and *Jaws*, *Picking Up the Pieces* really pushed the safety envelope.

He explains, "I had the challenge of hanging the actor with fireworks and then making sure he didn't get burned, and the crowd below didn't get burned, while still having a spectacular show."

Pieces has several fireworks sequences, including a Day of The Dead scene where El Torito – a man wearing a bull frame – runs wild through the town, spraying fireworks into the crowd. It was a dangerous stunt from any angle, so Surkin just decided he would do it himself. He may be the only special effects man in town who can list on his resume that he played the part of a bull in a film!

Another opportunity to dig down deep into his bag of tricks came with Florencio, a character confined to a wheelchair, who is seeking the healing powers of the Miraculous Hand.

"I had to build air bladders so that after the miracle cure, his legs would suddenly grow," explains Surkin.

Besides all the demanding pyrotechnics, the special effects coordinator was called upon to build a comfortable magic box to hold Sharon Stone while Woody Allen sawed her in half with a chainsaw.

"I had to make a chainsaw large enough to clear the box, but then the question was how to still have it light enough for a slight man like Allen to hold," recalls Surkin. "Then I had to find a way to safely run the chainsaw next to two people!"

Surkin has "Sliders" and "Scarecrow and Mrs. King" to his credit on the television side, and laughingly recalls a TV moment on "Everybody Loves Raymond" where he had to fly a plane through a window and land it on the bed — right as the star was about to become amorous with his wife.

Pausing to reflect, Surkin says, "I really feel I was born a special effects man, because I've been a tinkerer from day one. Born near the sea, I used to build boats and anything else I could get to float. I also loved to invent things that would help me catch fish quickly, then I'd take whatever I'd catch and sell it in the market."

Not surprisingly, the man who worked on *Jaws* spends most of his free time in, on, or under the water.

Some people are just born to their work.

Kelly Berry
Assistant Set Decorator/Buyer: *Garfield, The Italian Job*
Set Dresser: *Psycho* (remake),
among others

"The main thing that attracted me to this film was Director Alfonso Arau's knack for magical realism," explains *Picking Up the Pieces* Set Decorator Kelly Berry.

"Seeing Woody Allen as a butcher, wearing Wranglers and a Stetson hat, running through a village festival with the miraculous hand, is what magical realism is all about. It's the 'what if...?' game run amok."

In Arau's off-kilter comedy, this "miraculous hand" is associated with all sorts of mystical happenings, becomes very sought after, and eventually attracts the attention of the religious community. Coincidentally, church representatives arrive at the New Mexico village to validate the strange occurrences associated with the hand, at the exact moment the Day of The Dead festival is occurring.

"There was this huge celebration going on, at the same time we had priests carrying the hand through the village to be examined at the church," explains the set decorator. "So right off the bat, we needed to fill up the streets with miraculous hand merchandise, and simultaneously dress Day of the Dead festival vendors."

Berry recounts holding her breath, as she called all the way to Mexico City to find three thousand feet of authentic white plastic cutouts of Day of The Dead images, called papel picado.

"I crossed my fingers, and just prayed that it would arrive in enough time to string it across the streets during the festival. It ended up arriving only hours too late for parts of the main street, but it was here in time to put up everywhere else."

Berry had a great experience being able to work with Production Designer Denise Pizzini, one of her most supportive mentors, on the film. She is also very grateful for her team, and especially her Lead Man, Bob Lucas, and his great crew.

"There were such large and detailed expanses in the Mexican village, I couldn't possibly have done it without them."

Denise Pizzini, Production Designer
The Music Within, Like Water for Chocolate, Picking Up the Pieces,
among others

Ariel Award (Mexico) Nominations:
1992, Won (shared), Best Set Design (Mejor Ambientacion),
Como Agua para Chocolate (Like Water for Chocolate)

Every time she has worked with Director Alfonso Arau, Production Designer Denise Pizzini has experienced what it's like – to borrow the title of one of Arau's films – to take *A Walk in the Clouds*.

While finishing up work on Arau's *Picking Up the Pieces*, Pizzini explained, "The tricky thing about decorating and designing is that you have to be careful with your inclination to make everything beautiful. In a world where nothing is perfect, it can sometimes detract from the story. But I was so fortunate to be working with Alfonso Arau. He is known for his magical realism and he wanted everything to be gorgeous. So we were encouraged to add that mystical, surreal feeling to the sets."

It's often said that the third time is a charm, but Pizzini felt both lucky and charmed all three times she worked for the respected director. Before working on *Picking Up the Pieces*, she served as Set Decorator on *A Walk in the Clouds* and *Like Water for Chocolate*, which was honored for its set decoration with the Ariel Award, the Mexican equivalent of an Academy Award.

Pizzini spent her childhood at the drafting table of her father, an architect, and was often found "coloring walls." The artist went on to attend Texas Tech University where she studied interior design, and was designing an expanding chain of restaurants in San Antonio, Texas, when fate introduced her to Dorree Cooper. In town for production on *Johnny Be Good*, Cooper hired Pizzini as set dresser, and they ended up working on several films together, including *Fat Man and Little Boy* and *Honey, I Shrunk the Kids*.

In between designing restaurants and working for Cooper, the busy young woman worked as Art Director on commercials, and was placed on the list of the San Antonio Film Commission. Through a twist of fate, Alfonso Arau, with whom Pizzini was not yet familiar, got a hold of that list and called her to work on *Like Water for Chocolate*.

"At that time, I was seven months pregnant, and he was a director I'd never heard of, coming to me and asking me to do a million-dollar film shot in a small town in Mexico. To put it mildly, I was hesitant," she confesses.

"But he was willing to let me ship everything from Texas to Mexico, which meant I didn't physically have to be there, so I said yes."

Recalling the experience as "a low budget, Goodwill, Family Thrift situation with a few nice antiques," Pizzini remembers, "the way everything was presented, put together and photographed was so incredible, it just worked. And then we got the Ariel Award and we were so pleased."

Picking Up the Pieces centers around the transformational powers of a miraculous hand on a New Mexico town. The film opens in an ordinary world setting, but with each miracle that occurs, the town undergoes mystical changes.

"It was difficult as far as continuity is concerned, because there were about four phases of the town, and it wasn't shot in consecutive sequence," she explains.

One of the most interesting challenges for the designer was to honor the director's intention to pay homage to authentic Mexican culture while putting his own individual spin on things.

"We did a lot of research on everything, trying to combine a New Mexico style with old Mexico details. In the church, for example, we had a lot of murals and indigenous touches, and we put very believable vendors on the streets," recounts Pizzini.

"Then once we established that authenticity, we were setting the stage for the audience to be able to accept the altered reality of a miraculous hand."

Pizzini and her crew built all the interiors at Valuzet Ranch. "Some places we'd even use twice. The jail was also the rectory," she says with a laugh.

Cooperation was essential, and Pizzini reports that she has never had an experience where the various studio departments worked as more of a team than they did on that project.

To work with both Director Alfonso Arau and Academy Award-winning Cinematographer Vittorio Storaro on the same film was "such a thrill" for the artist.

"Vittorio is such a gentleman, and it was so satisfying knowing our work was in such good hands," she smiles.

Arriving at this wonderful point in her life wasn't exactly planned.

"I expected to pursue a career as an interior designer," she reflects. "The problem was that I didn't feel like I fit into the whole corporate design structure of working for clients, ordering mini-blinds. Then I discovered that I could apply the same skills to movies. And I knew I was so much better suited to this industry."

ANY DAY NOW

"Any Day Now" proves that life is rarely black and white. The ambitious drama is the story of a friendship that transcends racial barriers, and survives the passage of time. Set in Birmingham in the 1960s, the show uses variations of black and white and color as a metaphor for racial unrest and the simmering civil rights movement.

Heart-rending and poignant as well as historically revealing, "Any Day Now" is the tale of two little girls who managed to forge an enduring bond that, as women, they still enjoy today. Their innocent devotion to the preservation of their friendship, despite countless obstacles, turned out to be a very powerful weapon for change. All in all, this beautiful drama suggests that human warmth can be victorious and ultimately transformational, even in the days when segregation was the norm.

The episodes go from black and white with specific colorized props, to full color. They also skip back and forth between the beginning of the girls' friendship in the 1960s and their modern-day lives.

The workers agreed that these rich elements made for a television project that feels more like a film.

Mary Olivia McIntosh, Set Decorator
"Threat Matrix," "Any Day Now," "Townies," among others

On board with reality-based "Any Day Now" from its inception, Set Decorator Mary McIntosh was lucky enough to be involved in the conceptualization, design, and creation of all the sets, rather than having to step in mid-stream. The fact that the show, set in Birmingham, Alabama, moves from the 1960s to the present meant unlimited opportunities for creative fulfillment.

"It's been wonderful having the latitude to jump between the past and the present in every single episode. It forces you to stretch," she said.

Going in and out of filming in color also put an interesting spin on the process.

According to the artist, "When you're decorating in black and white, you're going in a totally different direction. You have to constantly be conscious of the issue of contrast, to make sure that every piece you bring on to the set will read in black and white. It keeps you on your toes."

On "Any Day Now," it was essential to simulate the look and feel of daily living, and give the audience the sensation that they just walked into the house next door.

"The best sets don't look like they're decorated," explains McIntosh. "They have a look of naturalness that is totally uncontrived."

The decorator notes that one of the keys to decorating is "layering for reality," and describes the technique as "putting big pieces and small pieces together, and then layering on top of that until a room has so much dimension that it brings you full circle back to what feels real."

If McIntosh's palette on "Any Day Now" was sometimes varying shades of gray, her life has always been very colorful. Growing up in Texas with "indulgent parents" who nurtured her creative tendencies, she knew, even as a young girl, that she would someday become an artist. Pursuing her education in art, she built her foundation on graphic design, and her approach to decorating is infused with elements from that discipline.

Her unique vision can be seen in such features as *The Electric Horseman*, the ground-breaking *Rumble Fish,* and *Cannery Row*. She also worked on the original *Free Willy* – an experience which left a lasting impression.

"If you've ever scratched a killer whale's tongue, it's not something you'll ever forget," she laughs.

The decorator, graphic designer, artist, and grandmother says she has a full and wonderful life and counts her many blessings. She also calls herself "very fortunate to have worked with incredibly talented people," not the least of which was her fabulous "Any Day Now" team. McIntosh says she's extremely grateful for her crew, and notes that they make her look good, which makes her department, the show, and everyone else look good, too.

She concluded, "Everything I bring to this industry comes from graphic design, my first love. Designing in two dimensions or three dimensions is essentially the same. It all comes down to the pictures in the back of my head, and how I'm going to bring those to life. Either way, my job is to take an idea and then go physically find what I see in my mind's eye."

Steve Desantis, Construction Coordinator
"Without a Trace," *Employee of the Month*, "Any Day Now,"
among others

Before "Any Day Now," Construction Coordinator Steve DeSantis worked on various types of projects as a Propmaker, from *Jurassic Park* on which he enjoyed building rocks and mountains, to low-budget TV shows.

"It's interesting going from *Jurassic Park,* where we had plenty of resources, to smaller shows, where we didn't have either the money or the manpower that we really needed – knowing they expected the same quality," the coordinator relates with a laugh.

"I learned different shortcuts and ways of doing things, taking into consideration what looks good and what doesn't, and what will and will not show up on camera."

Because the one-hour drama moves from yesteryear to the current day in each episode, the property master's eye for details and his refined aesthetic sense were especially important. According to the expert craftsman, it's an interesting and fulfilling challenge to shoot both the past and the present on a daily basis.

"Because of the changeovers required, we have to watch everything we do, from the door hardware to the differences in paint colors," he reported.

Color is a big issue on the show. As a metaphor for the

racial tensions that were so prevalent, the south of the 1960s is depicted completely in black and white, except for key pieces painted hot colors and then digitally colorized. The modern day scenes, meanwhile, are totally in color – using a different palette than the colorized pieces of the past.

When you add into the mix the architecture specific to that part of the country in both of those eras, it is understandable why DeSantis and his crew joked that "every episode is a small feature."

DeSantis said that helping him achieve "feature quality work on TV money" was an excellent, loyal crew that really understood when it was time to kick into high gear.

"Everybody on my crew, from the painters to the laborers, really puts their heart into everything we do," he said proudly.

Set in Birmingham, Alabama, the exteriors were shot in Pasadena, "except for some of the business district which is shot in Highland Park [California]."

All interior sets were shot in Santa Clarita [California], which just happens to be where the family man has lived all his life, and where he and his general foreman, Vince DeSantis, with whom he has worked for years, are raising their children.

The "Any Day Now" coordinator grew up planning on becoming an attorney, ended up working in outside construction, and only considered the studios after talking to a friend "who was building wagons and spaceships."

"It's been great," said De Santis. "I feel very fortunate because I've had steady work and made a lot of good friends. And I'm definitely much happier being outside than I would be sitting in a little cell of an office every day from nine to five."

7

The A-Team
Meet The Crews

Unlike the acting world, below-the-line studio work leaves no room for solos or monologues. It's all about teamwork.

Behind every great show is a perfectly synchronized crew. Department heads put together crews that they come to depend upon for years, and often take them from project to project.

In this chapter, the workers discuss how they rely upon each other, and the considerations and challenges of working in concert with other craftspeople and departments.

Loren Nickloff
Propmaker: *Erin Brockovich*
Construction Coordinator: *Trespass*
Construction Foreman: *The Goonies*
(among others)

Construction Coordinator Loren Nickloff was raised with an old-fashioned work ethic, and it served him well on "Thanks," a period sitcom based on the Pilgrims.

The show was a team effort between all the crafts.

"Every department, from lighting to set dressing, gave their input and offered their cooperation in brainstorming sessions," said Nickloff.

Following the old Indian adage that you can't know a man until you've walked a mile in his moccasins, all the departments put their heads together, and approached the project by learning to think like Pilgrims.

"We would get together and visualize everything, asking ourselves, if we were pilgrims, what would we do? How would we build furniture? What tools would we have used to make it, and what types of materials would we have had at our disposal?"

Nickloff and his team tried to recreate sets that the Pilgrims might have built, out of materials that they would have been able to find in the wilderness.

"That wasn't easy," explains the Los Angeles native, "since

the Pilgrims didn't have a lumber yard!"

That meant that all the departments had to be very creative, "like getting eucalyptus poles and palm fronds from the greens department to make thatched rooftops."

Or using plaster and straw that was aged to achieve the same look as the homes of America's forefathers, built by layering logs with mud.

The field of construction wasn't farfetched for Nickloff, who grew up helping his handyman dad around their house in Northridge. In his twenties, he crossed paths with a contractor, who broke him in slowly.

"He set me to work pulling nails out of lumber. I think he figured I couldn't get hurt too badly that way," he remembers with a laugh.

When he got it into his head to try to break into the studios, he didn't take no for an answer.

"The way I got in was kind of unusual. I went to the mill at MGM Studios asking for work, and they turned me down. So I showed up four days in a row. By the fourth day, they were getting upset," he says mischievously. "Finally, they hired me – on the condition that I promised to stay out of the office."

Nickloff served as Foreman on *Back To The Future II* and *III*, and then in 1990, after receiving his Coordinator's card, lent his talents to features like *The Doctor* starring William Hurt. He fully expected to continue down the feature film path – until he landed "Home Improvement."

"When I started on 'Home Improvement,' I stopped waiting for a feature to come along. It was a funny show – fast paced and interesting."

Different gags on the "Tool Time" segment every week provided so much stimulation and challenge that the craftsman was able to stay fulfilled and happy for eight years on the show.

And Loren Nickloff understands that on set isn't the only place that teamwork pays off, as he shares his Agua Dulce ranch with his wife and all the coyotes, rabbits, and other animals on the property.

"I really was born to work. Growing up I was taught 'work hard and you'll go places,'" he says.

Ray Maxwell, Construction Coordinator
Why Do Fools Fall in Love, Picking Up the Pieces, Romy and Michele's High School Reunion, among others

"The rain turned the entire ranch into a marsh. For the first couple of weeks, it was raining fifty percent of the time. Luckily, I've got the best soldiers around and it just came naturally to them," Construction Coordinator Ray Maxwell said, describing his crew's work on the film *Picking Up the Pieces.*

Despite the usual struggles with the budget, *Picking Up the Pieces* was a positive experience for Maxwell.

He calls Alfonso Arau "one of the most personal directors I've ever worked with," and says of Woody Allen, "For such a high-profile person, he sure is a down-to-earth guy."

According to Maxwell, he and his team were required to perform "a lot of face-lifting and other cosmetic surgery" in order to transform an existing rundown Mexican village backlot into contemporary New Mexico.

"There was so much structural construction that went into the overall project to make it a safe, shootable place. We had to take the existing structures, strip them down, and rebuild them to match the visual needs of the film."

One of the film's key scenes occurred in a church were the villagers have cornered the villain during a Day Of The Dead celebration.

"If you can imagine making a fixer-upper out of a church, that's really what we had to do," the coordinator recalls with a great sense of accomplishment. "We totally overhauled the interior and exterior, rebuilt the whole back lower structure, and then had to repair an entire stone floor."

Teaming up with a different kind of crew in the evenings, Ray Maxwell does a quick change from construction coordinator to musician. He even directed the first video for his band, Los Invisibles.

"I've always played in various bands, writing and recording my own songs and playing guitar," he says.

Putting his career into perspective, the diversely talented Maxwell muses,

"I always have had an artistic edge, so maybe it was inevitable that I would end up in this field. After all, as far as creative license goes, the motion picture industry is one of the most free."

Eddie Surkin
Special Effects Coordinator: **"The Division,"** *Picking Up the Pieces*
Special Effects Supervisor: **"Sliders"**
(among others)
-and-

John Roth, Special Effects Assistant
"The Division," *Guilty as Charged, Picking Up the Pieces,* among others

Special Effects Coordinator Eddie Surkin has been working with his assistant, John Roth, whom he met along with twenty-four other guys when they were all young adults in the now-defunct studio apprenticeship program.

Citing a tremendous wealth of knowledge and information found in his fellow workers, Surkin doesn't hesitate to call on them when needed.

"All of us from the apprenticeship program have maintained a friendship and, in time of need, we can draw on each other and pick each other's brains. John Roth and I have had an especially close friendship for the last thirty-three years. He backs me up one hundred percent and that's the most important thing."

Thinking back on how special effects have changed over the years, Surkin remembers that they had to work with a huge monkey for *King Kong*, and then a giant shark for *Jaws*, and points out that the hydraulics and electronics they were dealing with resulted in a breakthrough in that technology.

Surkin has a soft spot for Special Effects Coordinator Glen Robinson, who gave Eddie his break on the *King Kong* remake with Dino DeLaurentiis. He also fondly remembers Orien Ernest, Frank Brendel, Joe Goss, Carl Incorvaia and Doug Pettibone.

"I personally admire every single guy that came out of that apprenticeship program."

Gary Krakoff, Construction Coordinator
Independence Day, Freaky Friday, Monkey Bone, among others

"It's not just the drummer that makes the band valuable – it's everybody, the whole ensemble," states *Monkey Bone* Construction Coordinator Gary Krakoff.

"Our crew is definitely like a family. It's always a warm experience to come to work and see them. In fact, in addition to our work relationship, we actually share a friendship, going to one another's homes for dinner, and socializing on occasion."

Krakoff's band of talented craftsmen had some interesting and unusual assignments on the feature film, which combines animation and live action. A variety of full size and forced perspective sets were constructed on platforms, to accommodate puppeteers who worked the life-size Animatronics puppets from underneath the sets.

Heading up Krakoff's crew was Marco Campos, his general foreman. They have seen each other through the ups and downs of nearly twenty years in the business, starting out together as propmakers, going on to become foremen together, and eventually earning their coordinator cards. Together, they've lent their talents to such films as *Independence Day, Mars Attacks* and *Godzilla*.

"Marco and I have a really good partnership. We know how each other works, and that makes for one of the best working relationships possible; it doesn't get any better than this," Krakoff raves.

Welding Foreman and Fabricator Bruce Norrbom and Krakoff also go back about twenty years.

"Bruce has done a great job with a ton of steel sets – drawbridges, large steel platforms and structures. It's been the three of us for a long time," notes the coordinator who thought he would grow up to be a lawyer.

Krakoff has known one member of his construction crew since birth: Propmaker Foreman Gary Krakoff, Jr., with whom he also worked on *Independence Day*. Working together gives them the opportunity to make up for lost time.

"For all the long hours I worked when he was growing up, and all the time we missed being able to spend together, to get to see him every day is such a pleasure," says the elder Krakoff warmly. "He's a top notch foreman, and that's not just a biased statement made by his father. Anyone who has worked with him would agree."

For Krakoff, every member of his unit is a crucial spoke in the wheel. Propmaker Foreman Tim Lafferty always brings a great deal of expertise to the table; Charlie Serrano has overseen the location shoots as propmaker foreman, and Joseph Giorgianni, his long time finish carpenter foreman, does "all the intricate, complicated layouts, cabinetry, doors, windows, anything requiring compound angles."

Meanwhile Sammy Mendoza, another foreman, can add to his resume the fact that he built "Death's Office," and "The Coma Bar," two key *Monkey Bone* sets.

Wrapping it up, the coordinator observes, "There are so

many other people that are integral to my operation, I don't have time to name them all. Local 44 has a big pool of talented people and I've been lucky enough to get a hold of the same guys over and over."

Dan Pemberton, Construction Coordinator
Panic Room, Anna and the King, G.I. Jane, among others

When Dan Pemberton describes his work, he uses the old U.S. Army slogan, "It's not just a job, it's an adventure."

Pemberton, Construction Coordinator on the epic film *Anna and The King*, was an enlisted man at one point, but found the army wasn't all it was cracked up to be. He then spent some time in the logging industry in Oregon, before following his Propmaker father, Ray Pemberton, into the studios. Now his life is more of an adventure than he ever could have imagined.

For *Anna and The King*, Pemberton journeyed all the way to Malaysia. He was given only one day's notice that he had to leave on location.

"Getting to Malaysia takes forever. If you go any further than Malaysia, you're on your way back home," he teased.

Unfortunately jet lag wasn't built into the schedule. So despite a twenty-hour plane flight, the exhausted coordinator had to be rushed directly to the set so he could be brought up to speed. Driving down surprisingly good roads, he took in the sights of a whole different world. He saw the natives dressed in customarily modest garb, heads covered in scarves.

Once on set in the Far East, he was presented with an impossible deadline. The producers told him they couldn't give him any more time, but they would give him all the money and resources he needed.

Among the resources that went into the making of *Anna and the King* was an incredibly diverse crew made up of vastly different approaches, perspectives, and unique ways of doing things.

"It was really interesting to have everything on such a large scale and to have so many people working together," he notes. "We had nine hundred in our own crew and ten outside contractors building bridges, boats, and ships."

His team was made up of workers from Great Britain, Australia, New Zealand, South Africa, Thailand and Malaysia, and the eighty Local 44 members he brought from Los Angeles. They certainly had their work cut out for them.

He remembers, "We copied the King's palaces from Bangkok – they wouldn't let us shoot there – then we made everything twenty-five percent bigger and threw all of our assets at it."

The horsepower fueling the production consisted of fifty people in the Art Department drawing the blueprints, eight twenty-five ton cranes, a one-hundred-sixty-ton crane, and every piece of rental equipment they could get their hands on in Malaysia.

Finding the equipment they needed was no easy feat.

"I got out the phone book, and started calling everyone from one end of that small country to the other, from Singapore to the Thai border. I had every single scissor lift and condor they had," he says with a laugh.

They also occupied every hotel in Ipoh, where they would relax and regenerate over "very hot, spicy food that's like a cross between Chinese food and Thai food."

The construction crew had sets going all over the country, including the King's summer palace, for which they took over an entire island.

"As palaces go, it was just a small palace on the beach," Pemberton joked.

The building of the boat dock that went out to the ocean was occasionally sidelined by heavy surf.

Everything was a challenge, he recalls, because "there was no Home Depot and we had to search everything out." This was made all the more difficult because of the cultural clashes. While most of the Malaysians speak English, there are big differences in the way the language is used.

"It is a very laid-back country. We fly in, and we are the only ones in the whole country who are in a hurry. Then we try to explain that we have to find what we are looking for, and we have to find it yesterday. Only they don't understand our sarcasm, and they take everything we say literally. 'Yesterday? That would be impossible.'"

The propmaker's son appreciated his terrific crew, led by General Foreman Scott Mason, Plaster Foreman Mark Mancinelli, Paint Boss Dave Trevino, Propmaker Foreman Bill Slonecker, Labor Foremen Justin Walker and Ty Beck, and Toolman Jimmy Piccone.

"I had a great crew and I realized something very important. Without the guys I brought from L.A., we never could have gotten it finished. No matter what producers say, they're mistaken when they think they can go to other countries and get the same quality of work. The guys in Los Angeles are light years ahead of everyone else in terms of our work ethics."

He goes on to say he didn't play favorites, but gave his fellow American workers the toughest jobs of all. And they never once complained, but "out-worked, out-shined, and out-did everyone in every way."

Pemberton says that when he and his team arrived in Malaysia, everyone teased them saying, "Oh look, the cavalry's here."

To which he replied, "That's right. We showed up and we did the work and I couldn't be prouder. My crew did a terrific job and I appreciate them more than they know. The studio deeply appreciated their work."

Dan Pemberton has always liked to travel. And his career has given him plenty of opportunities to do just that. He spent a year and two months in Hawaii on *Waterworld*, and a year in Mexico City on *Total Recall,* where an average day included workouts in the gym, side by side with Arnold Schwarzenegger and Sharon Stone. Even after six months out of the country on *Anna and the King*, Pemberton was in no hurry to get back home. So he spent an extra month traveling around.

Among the high points for Pemberton were *Evening Star*

and *Devil's Advocate*, and especially his work on *G.I. Jane* for Director Ridley Scott, whom he has always admired.

Summing up the journey, he talks about other film greats he admires.

"It's been exciting to be around people I grew up watching on TV, like Vincent Price, Danny Kaye and Jonathan Winters. Ninety percent of the time, I look forward to going to work. It's better than most jobs because its always different. I'm building space ships one day and pirate ships the next."

Jackie Carr, Set Decorator
"Las Vegas" (pilot), *E.T., Jurassic Park,* among others

Carrying a loyal and invaluable crew, Jackie Carr has been blessed to have the consistency of a trusted team. Her Lead Man, Tim Donelan, has been her right hand since 1983, and her Drapery Man, John Slatsky, who has been in the industry for approximately forty years, has been with her "forever."

Carr has decorated many other-worldly films, many of which are Spielberg projects, including *E.T., Jurassic Park*, and *Twilight Zone, the Movie*.

She counts Spielberg and Robert Zemeckis as two of her favorite directors because, "They always know what they want and they tell you, so you don't have to guess."

Thinking of her own crew, the set decorator enthuses, "It's nice when you get a crew together that thinks along the same lines. It gets to the point where we don't have to talk anymore – everything becomes understood and unspoken. I know exactly how my lead man and my crew are going to handle things, and they know what I am going to do. It's great because we can all relax, and know we're there for each other."

8

Back To The Future
The Changing Face Of Studio Work

The way movies are made is constantly changing. When the film industry first got going, a star would be on contract to a certain studio and make all their films there. And at the studios themselves, everything was usually done in-house. They were, for the most part, self-contained, closed shops.

These days, it's not unusual for stars to work for several different studios, choosing the best script or the highest bidder. Studios open their doors so independent production companies can bring in their projects, and many productions leave town completely and film in other countries, like Canada.

Many free-standing special effects and prop houses now exist, and the mechanical special effects technicians find their work impacted more and more by the advancing technology in digital visual effects.

These are just a few of the ways that the face of studio work is evolving. But if it seems that nothing is certain anymore, there are some things that never change – a good story, which becomes a great script, and a memorable movie or television show.

Charles E. "Chuck" Dolan
Special Effects: *Traffic*
Special Effects Supervisor: **"Moonlighting,"** *Witness*
(among others)

"Movie making is different today," notes recently retired Special Effects Coordinator Chuck Dolan. "Years ago, they had more fun with the movies. We really had to use our imaginations to create an illusion. Now they're trying to do more realism, instead of creating an illusion. Now they want to see a guy actually burning up, or something exploding."

Charles Edward Dolan would know. Long before he ever became the founder of ASEPO (Association of Special Effects and Pyrotechnics Coordinators), served on the Executive Board of I.A.T.S.E. Local 44, or became a Special Effects Coordinator, the die was cast. With a mother who taught dance, and babysat for the "Our Gang" kids when she was a teenager (MaryAnn Jackson from "Our Gang" was a cousin); a grandfather who worked in MGM accounting, and a grandmother who worked as an extra and stand-in, it was no surprise that the young Dolan would make the movie studios home.

Growing up in Hollywood, Dolan remembers World War II taking the life of his uncle, a lieutenant; and then in 1948, he lost his father.

"After that, I went to work and never stopped. Cutting grass, trimming trees, and later working in a hotel in Yellowstone [National Park], doing dishes, working in the bakery, working as a fry cook. Then, in my spare time, I'd go from the Lake Hotel to the Old Faithful Hotel, and bellhop for tips."

When Dolan was about eighteen years old, the kid who used to mow lawns and trim trees – around his neighborhood that was filled with people who worked at the studios – was sent to work at Twentieth Century Fox on the wall gang.

Chuck Dolan remembers, "The first day on the job at Twentieth, I was asking, 'Where do I go? What do I do?' and the guy suggested we go to the commissary for lunch. I had packed my lunch so I left it somewhere, and there I was on the steps of the old commissary, and Lauren Bacall comes over and asks for a light. I was sitting there with my mouth open. I'd heard all the stories from my mom and dad, and there I was."

Working on the wall gang meant he would pick up walls and store them in the scene dock. He had to put the walls – it might be a storefront, for example – on a frame, then a tractor would pull that around, and a crane would lift them off a frame.

"That's where I learned to do rigging," he explains, "learned to tie stuff off, and learned how to lift walls without breaking them. Within two weeks, I was working on *South Pacific* with Mitzi Gaynor. It beat cutting lawns!"

Dolan notes that years ago, it was all about the actors.

"In those days, the actor – not the director – was the prima donna. We never would have turned a hose on an actor to get the effect of rain like they do today. We used to have rain pipes, straight across with holes on top, a half inch to three eighths across. We would turn the water on, and it would go straight down. Or we would wet the actor's clothing, and use glycerin to make it look like he was being rained on, but we made sure he didn't get wet."

"Or, if we wanted a dust storm," he continues, "we'd use our imagination to create something. We would use smoke and dust up the actor, maybe hit his hat so it looked like he was driving a herd of cattle. If we wanted an explosion, we would use directional mortars, a flash for a burst of flame, dust and cork. Now they just want fire. Now, the director may come up to you and say 'Hey, I want to see this guy on fire.' Or 'I want to see an explosion.' So they blow something up and dust gets into the cameras and equipment. In a way, they've lost the art of it."

Dolan talks about the lengths they used to go to so the movie going public wouldn't notice when they were flying someone with wires. They would use a stand of trees, all vertical, then a set designer and scenic artists would make sure there were plenty of vertical lines so you wouldn't see the wires.

"We used to create larger than life explosions on film that were no bigger than twenty by twenty," he points out. "We really had fun."

"This work is like being out in the desert. You're working your ass off for fourteen to sixteen hours a day, crawling for a glass of water, dying for some off time. But when you get that glass of water, it tastes great, and then after two days, you're ready to get right back to work. There's nothing like the satisfaction of doing a good job, and of doing something different."

The California native certainly never got bored. Working on *PT-109* about the life of John F. Kennedy is one of Dolan's favorite memories.

"We were in the Florida Keys, working with these mock-ups of PT boats," Dolan explains, " and we were out in the reefs and stuff, and it was so hot, you could walk into the water and hardly even feel it. There was so much coral, we had to wash our ears out with alcohol so they didn't get infected. Anyway, the PT mock-up would float in the water at a certain angle, to show that something had struck it and it was bent. It was great listening to the dialog, and following the story of how they were stranded for twenty hours in the water until they could get to an island. Then natives helped them get to where they had communication. Eventually, they got rescued. It was so weird, feeling so much a part of the story, and then the very next year, Kennedy was assassinated."

Dolan himself had many close calls, including one time on location when he got caught in a hurricane. He says that he and the crew saw about seven funnel clouds, and ran for the shelter of a concrete bunker with walls a foot and a half thick.

"It was probably only about twenty by twenty. The wind came up, blowing over the sets. It was touch and go for two or three hours. Some of the guys were praying. Then someone would carefully venture out, and then hurry back in. Then we had to all pitch in and re-do the sets."

If the hurricane didn't kill him, eating boxed lunches brought in from sixty miles away in hot weather almost did.

"The hardest thing about being on location," he jokes, "is that when you're working fourteen to sixteen hours a day far from home, there's no one to do your laundry. It was really tough back in the days before fluff 'n' fold. But being out there on the water, we sure came up with a lot of ways to cook fish."

Before the studios, Dolan worked at a nameplate company, an experience he remembers as totally monotonous. Bent over all day doing boring work, he tried to think of other things – like fishing.

"When I got studio work, that was it. It was like I went to Heaven. You know, if you don't enjoy what you're doing, it's work. If you enjoy it, it's not work. Every day was a challenge. Every day was great. I never look back. If something went wrong, my attitude was, 'What do we do now?' There's no time for blaming. Let's get it fixed. No time for regrets."

John Villarino, Construction Coordinator and Past-President (for six years) of I.A.T.S.E. Local 44
Minority Report, What Lies Beneath, Jurassic Park, among others

"Things are so different now," reflects Construction Coordinator and Local 44 Past-President, John Villarino. "The stars used to interact, and in fact, the bigger the star, the more he used to say 'hi.' Now, it's 'don't touch, don't look, don't be on stage with them' – unless they knew you from the beginning of their career. Then they see you, and they take comfort in a familiar face."

"I think in the beginning, these stars are very outgoing," he continues, "but the media makes them scared and reclusive. It's not surprising when you have fifty people screaming at you for your autograph, you can never go anywhere without getting hit on, and people have no respect for your privacy or your family."

Born in the Bronx, the former navy fireman grew up with the movies, and had "a whole fascination with Hollywood." Growing up on Long Island, Villarino remembers living in a neighborhood where there were so many houses that looked exactly the same, you couldn't tell your house from your neighbor's.

"My dad was coming home from work one night," he recalls, "after his first night on the job at the Waldorf Astoria, and there were like eight thousand houses – these slate shingle houses

– and none of them had numbers on them. He couldn't find our house."

Between playing baseball games, he was often found watching the classics, like *Ben Hur, Shenandoah, 12 O'Clock High*, and *The Godfather* movies, but he never imagined he'd get to work in the industry. Villarino sold cars, accordion lessons, and paint when he got out of the navy, until fate introduced him to a woman who would go on to marry a construction coordinator in the old studio apprenticeship program.

He remembers, "I was working at the paint store, and she was going with a guy who worked there, too. We ended up staying in touch because she was friends with my girlfriend at the time. Then she married Walt Hatfield, and one day they needed bodies down at Universal."

"I'll never forget my first day at Universal – it was wonderful. There were so many people there, I felt like I was in the service again. You had to go to the mill to get your assignment, and then drag your toolbox from stage to stage – I must've dragged that thing half a mile. But getting to feel the satisfaction of building something – that was great."

From "*Quincy, M.D.*" with Jack Klugman, he went on to *Airport 77* with a "tall, skinny, quiet" Jimmy Stewart, and never again returned to the world where you couldn't tell one house from the next. Everything was bigger than life. Like opening a door at Culver Studios, and almost knocking down Paul McCartney who was standing on the other side; walking into the men's room and having Glenn Frey of the Eagles walk in; or having water pistol fights with Marlene Dietrich's grandson, Michael Riva, on the set of *The Color Purple*.

"It was a brutally hot day on the set in North Carolina," Villarino remembers, "and there we were, spraying everyone with water. We were walking across rooftops, dumping pails of water on each other, squirting Stephen Spielberg with a water pistol. Even though it can become blasé because we're in it every day, we are living the magic life."

Among John Villarino's favorite memories is being personally thanked by Spielberg for building the sets for *A.I., Jurassic Park, E.T.*, and other Spielberg shows.

John Villarino has come a long way since he started at the studios, working with borrowed tools, earning a mere six dollars and eight cents an hour, which he says, at that time, was "three times more than anything else paid."

He concludes, "Everything is so different now, but that's life – the only thing that stays the same is change."

Gary Deaton, Construction Coordinator
Master and Commander: The Far Side of the World, As Good as It Gets, The Perfect Storm, among others

"We couldn't very well do heavy storm sequences with actors on a real boat – it had to be a controlled environment," explains Construction Coordinator Gary Deaton, "so we built an exact duplicate of the Andrea Gail."

A construction crew's dream, the ship unwittingly carrying her crew into harm's way had to be built to withstand some serious punishment. Given the sheer mass of the ocean vessel, and the fact that she got tossed, turned, and battered by a nightmarish storm, the film revolutionized the way movies are made.

The construction crew built the Andrea Gail in four sections on Stage 20 (at Warner Bros.) and then moved all four sections over to Stage 16.

"Then," continues Deaton, "we craned them on top of a gimbal, built by the special effects department, and welded it all together."

Constructed of steel and aluminum, and weighing in at one hundred thousand pounds, the boat was an astounding, impressive accomplishment. The coordinator describes the replica as measuring approximately seventy-two feet long and twenty-two feet wide.

Deaton continues, "It's a combination of platforms that had to be structurally engineered to stay intact on top of the gimbal.

The real boat was probably five times heavier, but since ours does sit on top of a gimbal, we didn't build the entire hull."

Built by the special effects department, the gimbal in question is an intricate piece of machinery, which required a high degree of collaboration between Deaton's crew and the special effects crew.

"It's not just a matter of us putting the sets together," the coordinator points out. "We had to be careful to do everything in the proper sequence, so the effects guys could make the attachment on the gimbal. And every time we made a changeover, we had to bring cranes on stage, do a lot of legwork, and communicate well with all the crafts departments involved. There was a lot more interaction than usual, because of the tight time schedule and the fact that what we were doing was very complicated and sophisticated."

In addition to coordination between all the local departments on the lot, the production also involved an out-of-town crew of carpenters, welders and painters.

Deaton notes, "I was fortunate to get such good people."

"The ship was big and I was very proud of it," muses the coordinator, "but I give the credit to my crew. All of them are very talented and conscientious, and they were able to anticipate problems before we even started construction. Many of them have been with me for awhile and they are a great group of men and women. And you know what? This was a tough movie, and we really had to think fast. The things we were doing were very innovative, but for as difficult as it was, it ran like a Swiss watch."

John Frazier
Special Effects Director: *Spider-Man 2*
Special Effects Coordinator: *Pearl Harbor, The Perfect Storm*
(among others)

Academy Award Nominations:
1997, Nominated (shared), Best Effects, Visual Effects, *Twister*
1999, Nominated (shared), Best Effects, Visual Effects, *Armageddon*
2001, Nominated (shared), Best Effects, Visual Effects, *The Perfect Storm*
2002, Nominated (shared), Best Effects, Visual Effects, *Pearl Harbor*
2003, Nominated (shared), Best Effects, Visual Effects, *Spider-Man*
2005, Won (shared), Best Achievement in Visual Effects,
Spider-Man 2

Academy of Science Fiction, Fantasy & Horror Films, USA – Saturn Award Nominations:
1999, Nominated (shared), Best Special Effects, *Armageddon*
2001, Nominated (shared), Best Special Effects, *The Perfect Storm*
2003, Nominated (shared), Best Special Effects, *Spider-Man*
2003, Nominated (shared), Best Special Effects, *xXx*

BAFTA Film Award Nominations:
1995, Nominated (shared), Best Special Effects, *Speed*
1997, Won (shared), Best Achievement in Special Visual Effects, *Twister*
2001, Won (shared), Best Achievement in Special Visual Effects,
The Perfect Storm
2003, Nominated (shared), Best Achievement in Special Visual Effects,
Spider-Man

Golden Satellite Award Nominations:
2005, Nominated (shared), Best Visual Effects, *Spider-Man 2*

Online Film Critics Society Award Nominations:
2003, Nominated (shared), Best Visual Effects, *Spider-Man*

Visual Effects Society Award Nominations:
2005, Nominated (shared), Outstanding Special Effects in Service to Visual Effects in a Motion Picture, *Spider-Man 2*

For John Frazier and his crew, *The Perfect Storm* will be remembered as their maiden voyage into uncharted special effects territories. Stretching the tried and true methods of creating special effects, the gargantuan undertaking definitely gave rise to ingenuity. The solutions Frazier and his department created to deal with a project of the size and scope of *The Perfect Storm* proved the old adage, "necessity is the mother of invention."

"In the past, what you gave the director was whatever it was. Nowadays, with the digital effects in the mix, everything is more complicated because we have to match our work with theirs — the type of waves, the way they break on the water — all of it has to be synchronized," explains the Special Effects Coordinator.

Working closely with digital effects company Industrial Light & Magic on the film brought up exciting new challenges for the coordinator and his team.

Frazier notes, "ILM was working on making hundred-foot waves, which were computerized and were going to look perfectly real. That made our job more complex, because we had to match their foam and everything they generated, and then do it in salt."

"The gimbal — which we made to run the ship — had a six-axis motion base with six rams underneath to control it," Frazier explains. "It was totally computerized, it revolved on top, and had one hundred thousand pounds of ship sitting on it. I believe that was the first time anyone made a computerized underwater gimbal that turned a complete three hundred sixty-five degrees so that the cameras could stay in one place."

Another frontier that Frazier and his specialists blazed on that production was having everything in the massive water tank float. The team was accustomed to bolting everything down and having it stay put, but the new technique allowed the floating wavemakers to be moved to where ever they were needed.

"We created different patterns, so the ship wouldn't always look like it was going in the same direction. As far as I know, that was the first time we had a motion base in the water," notes the special effects pioneer.

Frazier points out that digital effects have actually increased, not diminished, the workload of the mechanical effects crews.

"Scripts like *The Perfect Storm* simply wouldn't have been made if not for digital effects. I remember Steven Spielberg saying that he would make *Twister* as soon as someone could make a tornado he would like."

Shockingly, on *Twister*, Frazier and his crew dropped actual farm equipment from helicopters.

"We had to time it with the trucks moving towards the twister. We lucked out because that day, the sun was bright enough to cast a shadow from the truck, so you could pace yourself by looking down from the helicopter and seeing how much lead time you needed. Then I calculated how fast the combines and farm equipment would fall," he laughs.

The devoted father was assisted in such feats of daring by a loyal and enduring crew.

"I've assembled these guys over the years. They are all really good guys that work well together. And," he says modestly, "I know that I'm only as good as my help."

Randy Torpin, Propmaker
Jack the Bear
[worked on: **"Dharma and Greg," "X-Files"** among others]

Growing up in the cinematic environs of the [Twentieth Century] Fox Ranch, Randy Torpin had long had the inside scoop on how the movie business was run.

"Even as a kid, I knew how things in the studio were produced," he remembers. "For example, I knew there was no back to things – that everything was a front. I understood the craftsmanship that would go into making something look like a house when it's really not."

The Fox Ranch was the site of filming for "M*A*S*H," "How Green Was My Valley," "Love is a Many Splendored Thing" and many other films and television shows. Which made for a very colorful childhood for Torpin.

"We used to help out the actors. In fact, I remember one day when they were filming *Love Me Tender*, I opened my door and a wardrobe man was saying, 'Can this man take a shower, please?' The man was Elvis Presley, who was all wet and muddy from falling into a river," he says with a laugh.

It wasn't unusual for the ten-year-old Torpin's evening at home to include watching the studio workers make fog or rain or create explosions. He jokes that his mom would give him the choice between watching them blow up something, or watching TV.

Not only did he grow up on the Fox ranch, his grandfather and Fox founder, Darryl Zanuck, were first cousins. When young Torpin wasn't playing among the facades and sets or "helping out the actors," he was absorbing the skill and artistry that goes on behind the scenes. In his thirty-one years living on the ranch, he got the chance to refine his own talents and put them to work. From fix-it man to carpenter, he held many jobs.

Torpin ended up in the Fox Prop Shop in the late 1990s. Over the years since they re-opened the Prop Shop, Torpin and the other workers using the shop did any number of things – from standards, like breakaway furniture or welding handrails, to the space ship for the "X-Files," or an electronically lighted Golden Gate Bridge hat they made for "Dharma and Greg." For "Chicago Hope," expert metal workers made The Devil's Eye, a giant aluminum projector, twenty feet tall and fifteen feet wide.

Torpin and the other guys in and out of the Prop Shop at Fox enjoyed their challenges. The "X-Files," for example, kept them on their toes because when that show wanted a twenty-foot brass library ladder, they meant brass, not painted metal. And Torpin's crew delivered.

"The Prop Shop crew was made up of very sharp, well-trained, dedicated guys," Randy Torpin raved. "They didn't mind coming in early or working late. Their main job was getting the job done and getting it done right. Our motto here was 'Production Comes First.' That's what it's all about."

9

As Good As It Gets
The Little (and Big) Rewards

At the end of a long work day, or the end of an enduring career, everyone asks themselves, what was it all worth?

In this chapter, workers reflect on the rewards of a job in the studios. Some rewards are obvious, like nominations and awards. Or getting to work with favorite actors, directors, or producers.

And sometimes, it's the little things that make all the difference and touch our hearts. Like getting to work on a movie with your father, your brother, or even your son. Or the realization that you are living a charmed life.

Every life has its share of ups and downs. Sometimes things are bad, sometimes they're good, and sometimes, as the movie title says, they're *As Good As It Gets*.

William "Bill" Petrotta, Property Master
Bad Santa, The Rules of Attraction, The Thin Red Line, among others

"I have always been inspired by great directors, and I've been fortunate to work with some real geniuses," says Property Master Bill Petrotta.

"I was thrilled to work with Oliver Stone, a very collaborative man, on *Nixon* and *U-Turn*. And I also loved getting to work with Larry Kasden and Tim Burton — two more incredible directors. Those are the kinds of guys I get along with because they really bring you into the project. When you work with them, you're not just a guy hanging out. You're a member of the team."

The Santa Fe, New Mexico resident is the son, the father, the uncle, and the brother of Property Department men. He loves family. And he appreciates it when a great director or producer makes him feel like he's one of the family.

He got to work with his brother Vic on the *Perfect Storm*.

"The *Perfect Storm* was great for our department because there were so many props on that project. When you're on the boat, everything the actors touch or handle is a prop, and so is the boat itself," he points out. "And at least fifty percent of the film took place on the boat."

For the boating and fishing hobbyist, that film was the perfect gig. Employing a real-life, long-line fisherman as technical adviser, they simply followed along with the book.

Taking a real fishing boat off the coast of California for a research experiment, Petrotta says that no one had to twist his arm for that particular task. He wasn't exactly dragged kicking and screaming to the fishing village of Gloucester, Massachusetts, where exteriors were shot, either.

"I was so excited about that film," he remembers, "that I was getting up at four o'clock in the morning to go downstairs and read. The book was so good, I just couldn't put it down. And of course, I loved it because I own my own boat and I love to fish. I got to go to work in the morning and enjoy two of my favorite hobbies – boating and fishing. It was perfect for me."

"The characters were so well-defined in the book, there was no guess work," noted the property master. "The props were all spelled out for us. After all, things are what they are – a boat is a boat, a gaff is a gaff, and a fish hook is a fish hook."

"My job can be very challenging," he admits, "but I learn something new every day – because every picture has a different twist. Like on *The Perfect Storm*, I learned about long-line fishing. And on *Nixon*," he says with an ironic chuckle, "I learned about how the government works. I'm just glad that I'm not installing fenders at an automotive plant."

David Schwanke, Transportation Coordinator
The Break, Tollbooth, Breaking Point, among others

"Originally, I was planning to be a marine biologist. Then I came to Los Angeles for a summer job, made way too much money, and realized I could never make that kind of money in marine biology," says David Schwanke, Transportation Coordinator on "Jack of All Trades."

When Schwanke set out upon the short jaunt to Hollywood from Huntington Beach where he was raised, it was a road his father had pioneered before him. Now retired, Bill Schwanke also worked in the industry as a Transportation Coordinator. When the young Schwanke saw that Local 399 was advertising for someone to drive a lot tractor at MGM Studios, he didn't think twice.

Schwanke jumped in with both feet and spent his summer on a forklift, "moving lumber and anything else that needed to be moved" around the MGM lot. Soon afterwards, he joined Local 399.

"Back in those days, things were so much simpler. You just paid $50 and you were in the union. That was it," recalls Schwanke.

David Schwanke was not the only family member to follow his father into Local 399. The transportation bug also bit his brother, Paul Schwanke, Transportation Captain on "Jack of All

Trades." Harmony reigns where rivalry might exist between the siblings. The Coordinator speaks glowingly of working alongside his brother, calling him "a good guy and a really hard worker."

When we spoke, in addition to his brother, David's crew included a "hardworking, hard playing bunch of guys," like Dave "The Hammer" Moir, whom he called "a real character."

A people person, Schwanke reports, "The main thing that makes it worthwhile for me, is when the people that run a show and the members of the crew are good people."

"Jack of All Trades," about "a bad guy who gets tricked into a Wall Street scam and taken for some big bucks," was interesting for the coordinator because of the various locations where they were shooting, such as Orlando and New York City:

"The crews in New York were great, but Manhattan is a tough place to work. Between the crowds and the traffic, it was a challenge. I thought the traffic here was bad until I went to New York."

Like many things in New York, motorcycles "cost a fortune – probably twice as much as they do on the West Coast."

So, for a stunt where the hero is chased into an alley and has to abandon his motorcycle, Schwanke had to shop for the motorcycles in Los Angeles, and then ship them back to New York.

He happily took on the task, and says, "I loved it. It was one of the most enjoyable things I've done so far."

Other experiences that resonate for Schwanke are "Little

House on The Prairie," "Father Murphy" and "Highway to Heaven," on which he worked with Michael Landon, Producer Kent McCrae and Transportation Coordinator Clyde Harper. He calls McCrae and Harper excellent people who are really fun to be around.

When he calls to mind all the different people he's had the pleasure to work with over the years, Michael Landon has a special place in the one-time tractor driver's memory.

"He was definitely the nicest person I've ever worked with – he was just the best. Every good thing you've ever heard about him is true, and more. He was the kind of guy that would go out of his way to come and help you if you were in trouble."

While working together, Landon, McCrae, Harper, and Schwanke often arranged ball games to benefit children in crisis or need.

"We always had a great time, and it felt so good knowing we were helping those kids," Schwanke expresses.

Like many Californians, the would-be marine biologist is just as happy among the cactus as he is among the coral and fishes, and enjoys his spread in the high desert of Little Rock (California, not Arkansas) which he shares with his wife and three Akita dogs.

Of course, Schwanke makes room on the homestead for his vehicle collection.

"My wife hauls the dogs around in a Ford station wagon, and I'm just about to build a six-car garage," he said. "After all, I've got to have some place to put all my toys."

Paul Schwanke
Transportation Captain: *A Boy Called Hate,* "The Guardian"
Driver: *American Beauty*
(among others)

"It's been awhile since my brother and I have worked together, and I hope we can hook up and do it again soon," says Paul Schwanke. "I enjoy working with him quite a bit."

"Jack of All Trades" Transportation Coordinator David Schwanke, and Transportation Captain Paul Schwanke, have both been following in the footsteps of their father Bill, retired Transportation Coordinator.

Paul remembers growing up with a dad who was "always working."

"I went on a few shows with my father, and watched what he was doing with different aspects of transportation, and it all seemed pretty exciting," he recalls.

Years later, Schwanke got the chance to work with his father on the TV series "Fame" and a feature entitled *Endangered Species*.

One unforgettable day at Universal Studios stands out in Paul Schwanke's mind as the turning point of his life. It was 1976, and according to the Captain, Universal Studios was so busy, there were about twenty-eight TV shows and fourteen features all in production simultaneously.

"I showed up, and there must have been twelve hundred drivers in line to go to work. It was quite an experience. There was so much going on, and so many people there, I was in awe. I remember that I had lost my pen and had to go up to an older driver and ask if I could borrow his pen. He just looked at me and said, 'if you didn't come prepared, you shouldn't be working.' For years afterwards, I wondered whether he was serious or just teasing me."

When we talked, the transportation captain had recently finished *Fight Club*, and looking forward, hoped to find himself on board a project with his brother again soon.

T. Brooklyn "Tom" Bellissimo
Special Effects Coordinator: ***Dumb and Dumberer: When Harry Met Lloyd***
Special Effects Supervisor: ***What Lies Beneath, American History X***
(among others)

Visual Effects Society Award Nominations:
2004, Nominated (shared), Outstanding Visual Effects in a Television Series, **"Carnivale"**
2004, Won (shared), Outstanding Special Effects in Service to Visual Effects in a Televised Program, Music Video or Commercial, **"Carnivale"**

Tom Bellissimo attributes his success and good fortune to "the angel on my shoulder." Fate certainly seems to be smiling on the Special Effects supervisor, who has been leading the kind of charmed life you usually only see at the movies.

They say that everything in New York moves faster, but for this special effects man, it was his relocation to Los Angeles that put him on a rocket ship ride. Since switching coasts, his career has been moving at warp speed.

The Brooklyn-born magazine and book artist had no idea what was in store for him when, watching MTV one day, he fell in love with what he saw, and decided he'd like to work on rock videos.

"I started working in the art department on rock videos, and the next thing I knew, I was doing smoke for videos, and then getting called for smoke gigs from other video companies. Before

I even realized what was happening, I was being called a special effects guy," he says, incredulous.

Reflecting on the world of special effects in which he suddenly found himself, he observes with a laugh, "It's harder to float a pack of cigarettes across the room than it is to blow up a car, which is strange because people seem to cheer when you blow up the car and barely notice the cigarettes."

His new special effects moniker set into motion a domino effect, as he began to be brought on board for television shows, including "Werewolf," starring Chuck Connors, on which he turned union.

"When the opportunity happened, I took the bull by the horns and went with the flow," he explains.

He dedicated himself to voraciously learning everything he could about his trade, and ended up working for six years on "Tales From the Crypt." As fate would have it, his upward spiral gained even more momentum with that television series, which had at the helm a handful of the most well-respected and influential producers in film.

The Mask, Dusk 'Til Dawn, Desperado, and *American History X* were a few of the projects that came his way.

One of the "Tales From the Crypt" producers, Robert Zemeckis, remembered him for *What Lies Beneath*, which the special effects marvel refers to as "the hardest effects movie I've ever worked on."

Bellissimo teamed up with long-time partner Charlie Belardinelli, whom he calls "the best friend and partner anybody could ever want to work with."

He explains, "Zemeckis does these scenes that you wouldn't even know had special effects in them unless you happened to be aware of how he pulled off a particular shot. So you figure, maybe it will take twelve guys to do something that in actuality requires a team of twenty-seven," he reports.

One such moment came when a truck and boat were to go off a bridge and sink into Lake Champlain – in very shallow water.

"We had to sink a thirty-foot boat and a sixteen-foot truck in three feet of water. And make it look believable," he says, shaking his head. "So we did it in sections."

He has a wonderful team helping him pull off the miracles.

"I know that you're only as good as your crew, and thankfully, I have the best support crew and some of the smartest effects guys in the business working for me."

Beth Rubino, Set Decorator
The Interpreter, Analyze That, The Cider House Rules (among others)

Academy Award Nominations:
2000, Nominated (shared), Best Art Direction – Set Decoration,
The Cider House Rules

"I was renovating a hacienda in Mexico, so I had goats, chickens, and horses running through the set when I heard I'd been nominated," remembers Beth Rubino, who received an Oscar nomination for Best Achievement in Art Direction (Set Decoration) on *The Cider House Rules*.

It is no wonder that Beth Rubino received the nomination – the poignant and thought-provoking film would have been far less powerful if not for its exquisite visual backdrop. Thanks to its sheer beauty, *The Cider House Rules* managed to present controversial issues with humanity.

The film's success was due in large measure to its impeccable and seamless attention to detail.

"For me," Rubino says, "decorating is like a treasure hunt, where I'm looking for the needle in a haystack that will allow me to pull a visual thread through the entire film."

And when the New York-based Rubino thinks about *The Cider House Rules*, she loves the fine points the best – even those that never end up being seen on film.

Whether it is a hacienda south of the border, or the New England location where *Cider House* was shot, Rubino does not approach any project from the outside looking in. Complete immersion in an era or genre is one of her hallmarks. She loves saturating herself with the requirements that relate to a certain time period, whether it's machinery, technology, or the personalization of the characters.

"On *Cider House*, we set out to paint an entire socio-economic world for the characters. And that meant being cognizant of the fact that in those days, they were poverty-stricken. And I also had to understand all the medical instruments they used back then, and remember that they didn't have the luxury of technology. The whole depressed, pre-World War II era was fascinating," she remarks.

According to the set decorator, the pristine surroundings also presented interesting logistical challenges. Shot in three states – Maine, Massachusetts and Vermont – it required an enormous amount of research in order to achieve its high level of authenticity.

Achieving that seemingly effortless authenticity was a team effort between the artist and her "efficient and organized crew," led by Lead Man Scott Bobbitt. They sandblasted, refurbished, and augmented everything that was shipped back East from Los Angeles.

"Everyone worked very hard and they were a joy to be around," says Rubino. "You can't beat having people who work very hard and also make you laugh. My crew was abreast of the time period – all the lighting and wiring involved, and working with them was a real pleasure."

Beth Rubino has decorated many diverse projects, like *Money Train, Mumford, Sleepers* and *Twilight*. It is often long after twilight that Rubino slows down long enough to reflect on her life's path.

"Sometimes I'll be on location somewhere, watching a glorious full moon rise, and I'll stop and say, 'Oh my God, I really am blessed.'"

Andrea Joel, Set Decoration
"The Young and the Restless," among others

Daytime Emmy Award Nominations:
1999, 2002, 2004, Won (shared), Outstanding Achievement in Art Direction/Set Decoration/Scenic Design for a Drama Series,
"The Young and the Restless"
2000, 2001, 2003, Nominated (shared), Outstanding Achievement in Art Direction/Set Decoration/Scenic Design for a Drama Series,
"The Young and the Restless"

Along with Production Designer Bill Hultstrom and Art Director David Hoffmann, the Set Decoration team of Andrea Joel, Joe Bevacqua, and Fred Cooper was nominated in 2000 for an Emmy for their work on "The Young and the Restless." The team had received numerous nominations and several Emmys.

"It's such an honor to be nominated by your peers, and it is definitely a team effort," expressed Set Decorator Andrea Joel. "Every single person on the team is key, and I wouldn't even try to work without them. We also share our nomination with the property crew. There is no easy way to do a soap opera, and they are a godsend, making sure that day in and day out, everything runs smoothly."

Joel explains that in the world of soap operas, every day poses a new and different decorating challenge. In the space of a single episode, the crew may find themselves handling a range of real-life situations and walks of life – from a hospital to a prison laundry room to a street in Vietnam. Whenever possible, Joel, Bevacqua, and Cooper prefer to visit the places they are called upon to portray, instead of merely relying on printed research.

"For example," points out Joel, "when we had to do a scene in a Buddhist temple, we went to an actual temple, so we could speak with a real priest. Why go to a research resource when you can go directly to the source?"

Charlotte Garnell Scheide, Set Decoration
The Haunting of Seacliff Inn, "The Bold and the Beautiful,"
among others

Daytime Emmy Award Nominations:
1999, 2000, 2001, 2003, Nominated (shared), Outstanding Achievement in Art Direction/Set Decoration/Scenic Design for a Drama Series,
"The Bold and the Beautiful"

Along with Production Designer Sy Tomashoff and Art Director Jack Forrestel, the Set Decoration Team of Charlotte Garnell Scheide and Lee Moore was nominated in 2000 for an Emmy for their work on "The Bold and the Beautiful." The team has received numerous nominations and several Emmys.

Relates Set Decorator Charlotte Garnell Scheide, "It is a great honor to work with such a talented group of people. We are all team players supporting each other, so this is an honor for the entire group. We also bow to Bradley Bell for writing a show that allows us to really go wild with our creativity,"

Scheide explains that on a show like this one, where stories move and develop at lightning speed, and they shoot between thirty and seventy-five pages on a typical day, "there is always a myriad of things happening."

According to the decorator, it's not unusual for the crew to be contending with four or five story lines simultaneously. One character may undergo a quick decline from perfect happiness into the throes of a horrible disease. And at the same time, the crew may be called upon to depict a terrible plane crash in Iceland, while a torrid love affair takes place on an island vacation resort.

Notes Scheide, "We find our gratification in doing our research and paying close attention to detail, whether we are picking out linens or Italian lanterns for a restaurant scene. We put our hearts into making sure everything is appropriate for the locale, and even the food is accurate. That way, everyone gets something out of a project, and goes home fulfilled at the end of a day."

Scott Ambrose, Property Master
"Huff," "Any Day Now,"
Life of the Party: The Pamela Harriman Story, among others

Sometimes the reward for a job well done is a statuette or a plaque a worker can take home to his mantelpiece or hang on his wall, and sometimes the rewards of working in this exciting industry are more surprising.

One of the less obvious rewards is the richness and fullness of experience that goes along with working in film and TV. Like the benefit of having carte blanche to enter and explore environments to which the average civilian simply would not be given access. For at the end of a person's life, it is the richness and fullness of experience that he will savor.

This was certainly the case for Property Master Scott Ambrose when he was working on "Leaving L.A.," a short-lived but critically acclaimed series about the coroner's office. Believe it or not, Ambrose went so far as to study both with the L.A. Coroner's office, "researching how they investigated real deaths," and with doctors performing actual autopsies. It was on that unforgettable project that Ambrose was introduced to the producers of "Any Day Now," on which he became the property master.

Ambrose admits that the things that make him tick are the very same things that might push some people over the edge –

extreme pressure, impossible challenges, minute details, and complicated research. A born investigator, Ambrose abhors an empty blackboard. And the more complex and interesting the problem he is given to solve, the happier he is.

Eric Allard
Special Effects: *Spy Kids*
Special Effects Coordinator: *Home for the Holidays*
Special Effects Supervisor: *Stuart Little*

Academy Award Nominations:
2000, Nominated (shared), Best Effects, Visual Effects, *Stuart Little*

Academy of Science Fiction, Fantasy & Horror Films USA – Saturn Award Nominations:
1987, Nominated (shared), Best Special Effects, *Short Circuit*
2000, Nominated (shared), Best Special Effects, *Stuart Little*

Golden Satellite Award Nominations:
2000, Won (shared), Best Visual Effects, *Stuart Little*

Stuart Little, the story of the tiny mouse with the big heart, made a giant impression on the Motion Picture Academy, and also won a Golden Satellite Award for Special Effects Supervisor Eric Allard.

"I was very blessed to have so many talented people working with me," says Allard, "people that would run with my ideas, embrace them, and enhance them with theirs."

According to the special effects supervisor, he has always done his best work at Sony Studios. He worked at Sony on Natalie Wood's last film, *Brainstorm*, as well as *Short Circuit* and *Short Circuit 2*. Both *Short Circuit* films made it to the "bake off," Allard's nickname for the final round of consideration for Academy

Award nominations.

Stuart Little is the charming film adaptation of the popular E.B. White children's book. The story follows Stuart's struggle to fit in. Like Stuart, the special effects supervisor found his own niche by turning inherent difficulties in concentrating (ADHD) to his advantage.

What could have been a drawback became an asset when he opened his own special effects shop – back in the days when there were very few independent special effects or prop shops.

"Since it was hard for me to concentrate on any one project, I would keep ten projects going at the same time. Thankfully I found a bunch of great people, passed my ideas and concepts on to them, and with their help, I kept several balls in the air at the same time."

After fifteen years of running his own shop, the tides in the film industry began to turn. Allard realized he would have his best chance of continuing to work on high quality projects by closing up shop, and going back to supervising special effects for features. That decision led to Gabe Videla of Special Effects Unlimited recommending Allard for a small gig doing re-shoot work for producer Jason Clark. When Clark later went on to do *Stuart Little*, he remembered Allard.

Allard recalls, "I stayed right on budget, and also got to work with John Dykstra, who I'd respected for years. My crew was the best group of people I've ever assembled in my twenty years of working on effects."

Watching the industry go through many changes, the Special

Effects veteran believes that some things will never change.

"Just as acrylic paint may have replaced oils for some artists, there will always be those who prefer to take the classic approach. And it's the same thing with film. Just because new media has been created to replace film for telling a story with images and sound, there will always be people who prefer to work in an environment where actors can interact with people and props, as opposed to virtual environments and characters in a blue painted room. I don't think they'll ever do away with special effects altogether."

10
It's A Wonderful Life
Reflections From Retirees

So, how does it feel to have spent your life working below the line in television and films? We wind up our tale with trailblazers and industry veterans looking back at this privileged world.

This final chapter is a tribute to a few of those industry veterans without whom Hollywood would not have its incredible legacy.

It's A Wonderful Life: Reflections From Retirees

Luigi "Lou" Fasano, Propmaker
[worked on: **"Bonanza," "McHale's Navy,"** *Titanic* **(the original)**, among others]

"It was so wonderful to get up in the morning, go to work, and rub elbows with the real stars," recalls Propmaker Luigi "Lou" Fasano, who worked on the original *Titanic* for Republic Pictures [1953].

In a career that spanned half a century, Fasano had the distinction of having worked with Ronald Reagan, Roy Rogers and Gene Autry, "back when television really started coming in big."

He also got to experience the "Rat Pack" up close. Fasano recounts, "One time we were doing a Dean Martin western for Texas Films on the Universal backlot. Mr. Martin would be relaxing with a glass in his hand, while we were on standby waiting to change a breakaway window or door. Well, the tours had just started back then and every time a tour bus would pass by, he'd wave and yell things like, 'Keep sending postcards, we love you!' He was always cracking funny jokes."

One of Fasano's greatest challenges was for Ol' Blue Eyes. The propmaker remembers having to build sixty-foot circle platforms that would rotate as Frank Sinatra was singing. He was supposed to walk from one to the other in the middle of a song, and everything had to be exactly on cue.

"Mr. Sinatra would come in and check out our work, and we knew if it wasn't right, he wouldn't accept it. But he was always a nice guy to the workers. He was really the best."

Thinking back over the high points of nearly fifty years in the business, Fasano has especially fond memories of Danny Thomas from "Make Room For Daddy" and Maxwell House commercials, whom he remembers as being very warm and always making him feel welcome on the set, like family.

And Ernest Borgnine, from "McHale's Navy," who, Fasano recalls, "was such a sweet, lovable person. He'd be talking with the producer and the cameraman, and he would leave them in shock when he'd break away from them to come over to us and ask, 'Hey, what are you guys working on?'"

Born and raised in a large family in Italy, Luigi "Lou" Fasano came to the United States at the age of sixteen "because I wanted to explore America, and it was time to fly out of the nest."

Met at the train in Chicago by a member of the American Consulate who spoke both Italian and English, young Luigi experienced his first taste of America. And culture shock.

"I'll never forget it. They took me to a big department store in Chicago and said, 'You're going to have to dress like an American now!' I felt so embarrassed."

The world of carpentry and construction was in Fasano's blood. His father worked on the tunnels in Chicago, commuting back and forth from Italy doing construction, and his uncle was a carpenter at Warner Bros.

One of Lou's first jobs in the States was leaning lumber against houses for carpenters, until they went on strike. Then he found himself working for a few years in the grocery business.

"They were just about to make me a butcher at the market," he says, laughing, "and I didn't know if I'd like being in and out of the freezer, and having to cut the meat!"

In the nick of time, his uncle steered him toward the studios.

His sterling contributions to the industry include "Bonanza," on which he worked with Michael Landon, "Ironside" with Raymond Burr, and "Falcon Crest" starring Jane Wyman, with whom he had worked in his early days.

In addition to the film and television heroes he worked with, Fasano's resume reflects work with superheroes as well. His involvement with the "Superman" TV show for Warner Bros. and *Batman* left a permanent impression.

"The sets were huge for the *Batman* movie. We had to make windows for three-story or four-story buildings."

"In the olden days," Fasano recalls proudly, "we'd do everything by hand. Now they use a crane or a Condor to work on high stuff, but we used Black and Fall pulleys with ropes. We always made very high quality sets."

Fasano brought his traditional work ethic to pictures like *Dick Tracy* with Warren Beatty.

"It was very exciting and challenging because we hand-cut everything. Every single thing was made with our hands."

Arthur S. "Art" Rhoades
Special Effects: *The Old Man and the Sea,*
Captain Horatio Hornblower R.N.
Miniatures Supervisor (uncredited): *The Court-Martial of Billy Mitchell*
(among others)

The beloved retired Property Master Arthur "Art" Rhoades was around when the 1900s got rolling.

When I spoke to Art Rhoades, he was about to celebrate his 100th birthday. Throughout his distinguished career, he worked for United Artists, Paramount, and MGM, and was the head of the Property Shop at Warner Brothers for many years. He also has the rare distinction of witnessing the birth of motion pictures, and having a pivotal role in its golden age.

Admired and esteemed for his unique skills and talents, among the many films on his sizeable resume are *Ants, Captain Horatio Hornblower, The Call of the Wild, The Great Race,* and *The Old Man And the Sea.*

When I sat down with the legendary craftsman, it was hard to believe how many years had passed since his own "golden age." He was still vital, alert, active, and interested – and assisted by neither eyeglasses nor a hearing aid.

It was a very young man who first came to work in Hollywood. Rhoades quickly built a reputation as a phenomenon.

Retired Set Decorator Mowbray "Bunny" Berkeley relates,

"Anything you wanted, Art could produce – he was a genius. He could do prop shop gags that ordinary prop men didn't know anything about. Before you could even finish explaining what you needed, he'd say 'I know exactly what you want.' When you came back later, it was done. He was the most useful man in the business."

Flashes of memory, like cinema montages floating across the screen, remind Rhoades of career highlights.

"I remember being on a film with Edward G. Robinson where I had to make a knife that would slit open a shark so a man could fall out," he says and laughs.

Screen idols like Gary Cooper, Errol Flynn and Spencer Tracy, as well as moguls like Jack Warner and Bart Tuttle, were day players in the story of Rhoades' professional life. According to the property master, Gary Cooper was his favorite actor.

He spent time at sea with Spencer Tracy "eating abalone every day, and watching the sharks attack the boat that was carrying Tracy's double." At the mere mention of Loretta Young's name, his face lights up like a schoolboy's.

The property master is a quintessential collector who has lost none of his enthusiasm. Among his favorite possessions is an astounding collection of antique timepieces. Delightedly watching the second hand tick away, the legendary Arthur Rhoades revealed to me the secret that has kept him ticking for so long.

"Keep busy and never give up hope."

Cyril Poynton, Transportation Captain
[worked on: *Paint Your Wagon, Some Like it Hot, The Wizard of Oz,*
among others]

Driving. Flying. Swimming. For Transportation Captain Cyril Poynton, there were many ways to get from Point A to Point B, and he loved them all.

In addition to his many remarkable accomplishments in the field of motion picture transportation, the retired member was a master of the skies.

"I love flying," he admits, "and had a pilot's license for over thirty years." He would often jet off to China, Australia, or the Caribbean, and was said to keep company with such notables as Amelia Earhart and stunt pilot Pancho Barnes.

Poynton also had a reputation as a consummate swimmer, and worked as a lifeguard at the Ambassador Hotel on Wilshire Boulevard in Los Angeles before joining the union in the late 1930s. Long-time friend and fellow retiree Al Schultz worked with Poynton for about fifty years, and recalls:

"Cyril always loved to swim, just like his sister. He went for a swim every day before work, regardless of how cold it was outside."

Poynton's sister, Dorothy, was the youngest American to ever win an Olympic medal, when she took the bronze in springboard diving at the age of thirteen. She went on to win two gold medals and another bronze, between 1928 and 1936.

Growing up in Ogden, Utah, Poynton and his siblings were taught a strong work ethic. On school days, young Poynton spent so much time collecting newspapers to heat the classrooms, that school was almost over by the time he had finished his task and was ready to hit the books.

Life is often the best teacher, and what he missed in academics, he picked up along the way. One thing that the driver learned early and learned well was the importance of knowing how far he would go – and when to stop.

"One time I was driving someone to location and he kept pushing me to drive faster. I told him if he didn't like my driving, he could get out of the car. He did, and I drove off," he recalls with a chuckle. "He made it a point not to get in the car with me again after that."

Cyril Poynton joined Local 399 before World War II and thanks to union benefits, has been happily retired for years.

"While I was still working, I always enjoyed the [union] brotherhood. And I understood that the union was important so that employers don't take advantage of workers. I appreciated the health benefits, the guaranteed fair wages, better working conditions, and retirement planning," he says.

Now, having retired over twenty-five years ago, he enjoys the guaranteed income and healthcare.

There was a long stretch of road between when Transportation Captain Cyril Poynton first started driving, and when he put away his driving gloves. In the beginning, he worked for forty-two cents an hour with no overtime pay. And half a century later, he retired as a beloved and distinguished transportation captain, with a life so full it would take several rolls of film to tell his story.

In the long span of his illustrious career, Poynton worked on such classics as *The Wizard of Oz, Some Like It Hot,* "Route 66," *Paint Your Wagon,* and variety shows with Bing Crosby, Bob Hope, and Sonny & Cher.

For every mile there is a memory. And for every straight and narrow, there were many turns in the road – the most surprising of which was the career itself.

"In those days," he reflects, "there was no time to think of what I wanted to be when I grew up. It was too hard just to live."

Working the pedals from the floorboards while W.C. Fields drove the car. Chauffeuring Marilyn Monroe and John Wayne. Working with Bing Crosby and Bob Hope, whom Poynton calls "a real gentleman." Delivering the Matterhorn to Disneyland. Driving the first electric car.

The 92-year-old Poynton sums it up by saying, "It's been a hell of a ride."

Chuck Gaspar

Special Effects Supervisor: *Beetlejuice*
Special Effects Foreman: *Armageddon, Twister*
(among others)

Academy Award Nominations:

1985, Nominated (shared), Best Effects, Visual Effects, ***Ghostbusters***

The son of Propmaker Geeza Gaspar, Special Effects Co-ordinator Chuck Gaspar grew up in Downey, California, as one of three children. At seventeen, he volunteered for the Army.

"When I got out, I worked for my brother-in-law, selling vacuum cleaners, but that was a bummer. One day my dad called me to go to work for the studios. I remember that I only worked for 28 days, and then I got a pink slip. I asked him, 'laid off? What in the world does that mean?'"

The same thing happened on his next job for MGM – twenty days later he found himself laid off. Thinking to himself, "This is a crazy business," he went to work in the tool and die industry. The tides turned when a friend of his father's called him to go to work on the Universal film *The Birds*.

"My first day, I showed up to work for Larry Hampton and I said, 'If you're going to lay me off, do it today.' Lucky for me, he said, 'Don't worry, Chuck, you're on and this time, you're not going anywhere.' So thank God, it worked out."

Always willing to go to any lengths for his craft, Gaspar has found himself in some unlikely roles.

"I developed the unusual skill of taxidermy on *The Birds*," he recalls, clearly amused. "There was a scene where Tippi Hedren was driving with two canaries that I'd had to stuff in three hours time, and then put back in their cage. It was wild."

After garnering an Academy Award nomination for his work on the first *Ghostbusters* film, special effects coordinator Chuck Gaspar went on to work on *Ghostbusters II*, an experience he's not likely to forget.

"We were shooting in the middle of Manhattan, with a crane that held up a huge bag of shaving cream that was supposed to look like marshmallow cream."

As luck would have it, the very moment Gaspar was called away from the set, a workman told the lead actor, "You better watch out, that bag weighs a ton and it's going to fall on you."

"After he'd said that," Gaspar laughs, "I realized I had no choice but to stand under the bag, and let the shaving cream fall all over me so the actor would know he wasn't going to get hurt."

The special effects coordinator had a long and fulfilling career, and a list of credits of which anyone would be proud. Particularly memorable for Gaspar was working with Tim Burton (*Beetlejuice*) and Clint Eastwood (*Pale Rider*), whom he calls "two of the best directors I've ever worked for."

"It's funny – Eastwood is basically just like he is in his films. He doesn't talk much and he's very, very cool."

Pee Wee's Big Adventure also stands out in Gaspar's memory, because he and his crew had their own adventure – a very close call, with a Hollywood-style happy ending. They were called upon to make it look like Pee Wee [Herman] was flying through the air, and over a house on a bicycle.

"We put the bike on a cable between two cranes, and had a ramp on the other side of the house. And I swear we must have set up eight hundred boxes, to catch the rider in case he dropped off prior to when he was supposed to. Would you believe, he missed every single box. Eight hundred boxes and he missed them all! What a ride that was." The coordinator shakes his head, reliving the moment. "Thankfully, the rider wasn't hurt."

In 1998 after nearly 40 years of work, the industry veteran finally put down his tool box and decided to take a gamble on life in Las Vegas.

"The up side is that I can take my boat to Lake Mead which is only 45 minutes away, or take my dogs and head up to Lone Mountain in my four-wheel drive. And the downside is that… well, let's just say it gets a little warm here," he grins.

Clyde Harper

Transportation Coordinator: ***"Highway to Heaven,"***
Little House: Bless All the Dear Children
Transportation Captain: ***Paper Moon***
(among others)

After working for nearly seventy years, Clyde Harper has finally pulled off the road to rest.

The Driver and Transportation Coordinator with the enduring career first got behind the wheel in the thirties. He was seventeen years old and the world looked very different.

"We didn't even lock the doors or windows back then," Harper wistfully recalls.

One of the original Teamsters, Clyde Harper began his long haul as a commercial driver.

"I started when the unions were just getting going, and from the very beginning, I knew how fortunate I was to be a Teamster. I saw people that didn't belong to the union, and the way they were treated. In fact, when I was driving from Los Angeles to Chicago, there were drivers from 'right to work' states who were driving the same equipment I was and carrying the same commodities, but only earning half the pay."

Prior to joining Local 399, the driver worked for Santa Fe Trailways (now Continental) and then switched to driving long distance trucks for Consolidated Freightways. He remembers doing a sleeper route from Los Angeles to Seattle, when there were a lot of two-lane mountain highways that weren't banked like they are now.

"By the time you got far enough north to hit those two-lane roads, there was so much ice and snow, and so many hazards, you'd have no problem staying awake," he jokes.

The late 1950s found Harper out of work, as his union went on strike. So Harper called a friend – a fellow long-distance driver who had discovered the gold-paved streets of Hollywood. He was immediately given a job with a trucking company that furnished equipment to the motion picture industry. Soon afterward, he became a card-carrying member of the union.

"Local 399 has been very good to me. They have great agreements, and they have always taken real good care of their membership," the coordinator raves.

The transportation coordinator worked with Michael Landon for nearly forty years. Starting out on the original "Bonanza," they also worked together on "Little House on the Prairie," and "Highway to Heaven."

His years with Michael Landon were a joy.

"He was the greatest guy in the world, and he treated everybody like a king. Nobody ever quit working for him, so there was rarely an opening."

Landon was so gracious as to allow Harper to work on other features, and then return to his job which had been held open for him.

When he wasn't working with Michael Landon, the industry veteran worked on such star-studded pix as *Swingers* with Ann-Margret, *The Out of Towners* starring Jack Lemmon, and *The Sons of Katie Elder* featuring John Wayne. During the making of *Katie Elder*, John Wayne had to have a serious operation.

The coordinator relates, "We were all shocked when he bounced back right away, and showed up on the set so soon afterwards. In real life, he was rugged, just like he was in the movies."

One of the rewards of such a long run in the entertainment industry is a treasure chest of unique remembrances. Like the time he took a young Tatum O'Neal trick-or-treating, while working on *Paper Moon* with her and her father, Ryan O'Neal. Or the time he got to work on *5 Card Stud* with two classic leading men of the old tradition – Robert Mitchum and Dean Martin.

"They were a lot of fun to work with; really great down-to-earth guys."

The coordinator has a deep appreciation and fondness for all the great guys and gals he's had the pleasure to work with over the decades.

"The reason I was able to be so successful in the business was that I could always recognize good drivers," he notes. "All my drivers were top people."

The Los Angeles-born Harper has seen a lot of this fair country, and has traveled abroad as well. Three children and six grandchildren later, the transportation professional was still going strong when we spoke.

Harper once worked on a movie called *The Immortal*. In that film, the hero was pursued by those wanting to know his secret so they could live forever.

Asked if he has any tips for a long life, he says, "Behave yourself and believe in God." Amen.

Frank Hafemann,
Construction Coordinator and Special Effects Technician
[worked on: *The Greatest Story Ever Told,* "The Lucy Show," "Star Trek," among others]

It was when a tornado wiped out seven barns in a thirteen-mile stretch in Frank Hafemann's hometown of Green Bay, Wisconsin, that he first learned carpentry. Growing up on a dairy farm, Hafemann helped support his family by chopping their sugar maple trees into firewood – which they sold for $3.50 per cord.

He would go on to fish on his uncle's houseboat on the Mississippi River, work in a sawmill, cook in his mother's restaurant, and tend bar, before having another chance to work with wood.

In the early 1940s during World War II, the young Hafemann's skills were sharpened further. For health reasons, he was not permitted to enlist, but he did his duty by building barracks at various army camps.

"They were desperate for anyone who could hammer a nail, so I learned a lot of carpentry pretty quickly," he recalls.

Following a friend's lead into the movie studios at the end of the war, the farmer became a construction coordinator who also worked in special effects. After a youth spent hard at work, Hafemann began to make history in Hollywood. He did special effects for such favorites as "The Lucy Show" and "Star Trek." And in his spare time, he taught the nine-year-old daughter of a friend to ride horses.

"She became a good rider. And a movie star – Natalie Wood."

He worked on *Rio Bravo* and *The Cowboys* with John Wayne. His efforts on *The Hallelujah Trail* paid off, when the same art director took him for eight months to idyllic Oahu for the shooting of James Michener's *Hawaii*. Hafemann also worked on the popular "Mannix" and "Mission: Impossible" TV series.

While en route to Los Angeles during the filming of *The Cowboys*, a friend promised an introduction to a wonderful woman who lived in Santa Fe. Within a year, Jean became Mrs. Frank Hafemann and in 1973, they settled in Santa Fe. Two days after their marriage, Hafemann had to fly to Georgia to work on *Conrack*, which received an Academy Award nomination for its sets.

Throughout his many years in the industry, Frank Hafemann lent his magic touch to many of the best known and best loved films and television shows. And his life took on a surreal quality.

Thinking back to *The Greatest Story Ever Told*, he remembers, "I had to nail full-sized latex bodies to crosses. When I hit the nails, the bodies would jump and shiver. It was eerie."

Several years ago, after many wonderful years and great adventures together, Frank lost his dear wife, Jean, but he stays close with his children and grandchildren. Drawn by the lush green hills of Oregon, he recently moved to the small town of Brookings, where he is making new friends. An avid fisherman, he enjoys living so close to the ocean. Looking out at the many flowers that the Oregon rains keep in bloom, he says he's growing fond of his new home. Frank Hafemann's youngest son, Alan Hafemann, works as a propmaker/prop shop person.

Lawrence "Larry" Needham,
Special Effects Technician
[worked on: *Jaws 1, 2* **and** *4, The Chase,* **"Bewitched,"** among others]

"I don't remember learning to walk, and I don't remember learning to swim. They tell me a dog pushed me off the end of a dock and I came in all wet," recalls Larry Needham.

Growing up in Rhode Island, the special effects technician who worked on *The Islands,* and *Marooned*, has always loved the water.

As a kid, he spent most of his free time fishing. Years later, he would end up building the sharks for the *Jaws* films and for the Universal Studios Tours. And bringing home sharks tooth necklaces for his kids.

"When we made the first sharks, we made them out of regular metal," he explains. "Then after you stick them in salt water, they get totally ruined. So for every movie, you have to make more sharks. We built the sharks for the tours out of stainless steel, because it's harder than plain old iron."

Needham spent the first several years of his life in New England, and when he was six years old, a big hurricane blew through town. The young man who would one day learn to create wind and rain, and alter movie weather at will, almost didn't see seven years old.

"I was in the first grade at school," he remembers, "and the leaves were really blowing, so the state trooper told us to go home. We were driving across the bridge out of town, and I was watching big chunks of roof flying around. One of the roofing nails got stuck in our tire. I was sitting in the backseat of our car and I decided I'd get out and help my father fix the flat. Well, the wind blew me off like a tumbleweed, up against a chain link fence. My dad had to crawl on his hands and knees to get me. Somehow we all made it back into the car."

He walked the last mile home after the eye of the hurricane had passed, then the wind came up again, and he saw their apple tree disappear right out of their yard.

Not long after his tangle with the hurricane, World War II hit. So his father – who had been working in construction, helping to build the Empire State Building – took the family, moved them to Southern California, joined the war effort, and gave his son a longing for the West Coast that never left him.

The family returned home to New England after the war, but then a teenage Larry Needham took some pocket change and left home again, thinking he might get work on a Florida fishing boat. He ended up living on his uncle's Southern California chicken ranch, and working at the racetrack. After one more trip back East when his father developed lung problems, Needham – along with his parents, this time – was soon back in California, for the dry weather. And for good.

Eventually, he picked up a hammer and followed his father

into construction work. In the early 1960s, the divorced Needham, who was a member of the carpenters' union, met and fell in love with a girl who had worked as a messenger girl and a production secretary at the studios.

Not long after they married – and he became a father to her three young children, and soon after, they had twins – the construction work he'd been doing started to slow down. With five young mouths to feed, he needed steady work.

He recalls, "My wife said to me, 'You know, the studios use carpenters. Why don't you go down to Local 44 and see if they're hiring?'"

When he got to the union hall and started filling out the application, they discovered he could weld. And so the die was cast for the carpenter to work in special effects.

"They had a lot of work, building some big steel framework for cannons or something, and I arrived with nothing but a tape measure," he recalls, shaking his head. "When they had called me to come in, someone told me, 'Oh, don't worry, they'll supply everything.' So I reported to the special effects department and they said, 'Where's your toolbox?' I held out my tape measure and said, 'This is all I have.'"

He soon learned how to put his experience as a carpenter to use on more unusual challenges. Like making a train and train tracks out of laminated plywood for the series "The Iron Horse."

"It's been such interesting work," reflects the special effects veteran. "For example, one day, someone wheels in a brand new Cadillac with only seven miles on it. There's a person inside the car holding the steering wheel, and we take off the front of the car. To cut up a car like a jigsaw puzzle – so you can open the door, pick it up and walk off with it – it's very detailed work."

Working on "Bewitched," there was a scene where the uncle is hiding in a closet and he had made himself invisible.

"In the storyline, he'd forgotten to make his shoes invisible," explains Needham, "so they wanted a pair of shoes to walk out of the closet. There was a way of having an actual person walk out of the closet and then erasing the person, but it was an expensive procedure, so we started experimenting."

Using color-safe piano wire and sticks stuck inside the toe and heel of each shoe, Needham went twelve feet up in the air and put up a plank that would match the floor, so he could move along the plank, and walk the shoes, matching the line from the closet door to the front door.

"The only thing was, when I got up there, I realized it was impossible to see to both to the left and right of the plank at the same time, unless I walked along a two-inch- wide plank, walking sideways and bending forward. So I held the two shoes and the wires appropriate space apart, and watched the shoes going heel, toe, heel, toe, all while walking sideways and not being able to see where I was going."

Needham learned pretty quickly what a dangerous world the arena of special effects can be. Once, he was even thrown from a ladder with a drill motor in his hand.

He explains, "I was working on the *Incredible Shrinking Woman*. Now, if you're going to make a tiny, shrinking woman, you have to make everything else big, so we had a twelve-foot hamster cage out of metal."

They had the wheel for the hamster cage and the bars, and then they had to rivet the metal in place on top of the cage. Since it was twelve feet high, they had to take a ladder and lean it up against the sheet metal going up the side of the cage, and then take a drill motor up to drill the holes.

"When you go up a ladder," Needham points out, "you set the rubber feet on the floor and lean it against something. Then you tentatively go up and make sure it's secure."

All morning, he had been going up and down the ladder, carrying rivets and drill bits, and he had become very confident.

"It got to the point where I was actually running up and down the ladder. Then we went to lunch. And when we came back, I ran up the ladder, and something wasn't right. When I looked down to see the rubber feet, I realized the ladder was upside down."

As he went sliding down the ladder, he tried to throw the drill motor away and grab one of the rungs with both hands. He missed the rung, and his wrist caught under it when it hit.

"I jumped up," he remembers, "and yelled, 'Hey! Who turned this ladder upside down!' A guard said a forklift had wanted to come by, so he moved it, but he put it right back. Yeah, he put it back all right – upside down!"

Many years later, working on *Jaws*, Needham found himself on Martha's Vineyard, being reminded of the hurricane incident.

"They needed me for some reason – something was busted on one of the sharks – and all the hotels were filled up. The only accommodation they had for me was a room in some lady's house. It was totally unacceptable – nothing but a bed and chair. No TV, no radio."

They promised Needham that as soon as a room became available in one of the hotels, they would let him know, so every night after work, he'd stop in and talk to the production secretary to find out when he was going to get a room.

"One night," he remembers, "she finally says, 'We've got a room for you. The airline pilots just informed us that there's a hurricane headed this way, and if the hurricane is definitely going to hit this island, they're leaving. You can have one of their rooms.' I told her, 'Don't worry, if those pilots leave, I'm leaving with them. I've been in a hurricane before!'"

He concludes, "It's very satisfying to realize you brought so much entertainment to so many people's lives. Not that the movies and TV were the high point in their lives, but maybe we made life a little less bleak."

Afterword

Who are we? How do we touch other people's lives? We are carpenters that build space ships, and control enough electric power to light up a whole town. We bring fears, jeers, tears, debate, and the whole range of emotions to everyone who has ever watched a movie or TV show.

It's hard to believe that a hundred years ago, you had to watch moving pictures for a penny, on a two-inch or three-inch screen that you had to hand-crank. Then came silent pictures where scenery was dull and gray, everybody who looked good was good, and theatrics were king. Forward-thinking men figured there was money to be made with a new studio system where contracts were honored and, for actors and crew alike, it was a well-paying vocation. Sound made and destroyed careers en masse, both in front of and behind the cameras.

In the old silent film days, you could film outside in the street on a carousel. You could turn the set to the sun, talk over each emotion or theatric, and tell the people what to do. With the advent of sound, you could hear grips moving equipment, trucks idling, and background noises – like people yelling and trains passing by. Yes, sound made and destroyed careers. Now, instead of sets on the street, we need big boxes – stages – and since we're not outside, we need lights and different cameras and film. The upside is since we are inside, we have much more control over everything – we can make it light or dark, we can make it snow and rain at will.

When the old studio system was replaced by star-and-agent-hour, it was as if the lunatics had control of the asylum. Huge budgets and huge blockbusters created a vibrant and wealthy business, and gave rise to a time of excess and power.

When TV was first invented in the fifties, it almost annihilated the movie industry, because everyone was watching at home, but the truth is, TV will never stop us. That's why Vista Vision and other new processes were invented – things like wide screen formats, Cinemax, Imax – to get people away from their TV sets and into the movie houses. That also explains why the movie palaces of that era were so beautifully done – to get people to go out to the movies again. TV was behind the demise of the old studio system, because with TV causing attendance at the movies to drop sixty percent, the studios could no longer afford to keep actors on the payroll.

Now TV owns film. Networks own the movie lots. TV was a negative factor for the movies, but eventually gobbled up the major studios. Then worldwide economics and the shrinking dollar drove business away from Hollywood – it became cheaper to film elsewhere, because the dollar could buy so much more overseas, and that's why we now have what's known in Hollywood as "runaway production." Economically speaking, it became cheaper to make this a worldwide business where profits were even greater, and today this little business is a worldwide conglomeration, with thousands of companies, and payrolls and profits in the billions of dollars.

In the 1950s, the movies kept getting bigger and bigger and bigger. Now, we're getting smaller and smaller. We went from black-and-white silent pictures to full color Vista Vision, to color two-inch or three-inch screen pictures – that's right, with the advent of CDs and DVDs, you can watch movies again on a two-inch or three-inch screen in your hand. It's a color talkie movie just like in the beginning, only now you don't have to hand-crank, you just sit back and enjoy.

We have come full circle.

*– John Villarino, Construction Coordinator
and Past-President of I.A.T.S.E. Local 44*

And a few last words from your Author...
(Or, if that was the AFTERWORD, this is the LASTWORD)

I recently had a chance to catch up with Special Effects Supervisor T. Brooklyn ("Tom") Bellissimo, whom I first interviewed between 1999 and 2000. Tom and his partner, Charlie Belardinelli, won the 2004 Visual Effects Society award for Outstanding Special Effects in Service to Visual Effects in a Televised Program, Music Video or Commercial, for their work on the Pilot for HBO's "Carnivale." The special effects pair also star in the reality-based "Boom!" which is an Original Productions show currently airing on Spike TV.

Our conversation made me think about The Big Picture – how big pictures on screen make us think differently about the big picture of life.

When we talked, Tom was at work on HBO's "Carnivale." The show is set in the dust bowl era, and centers around a traveling carnival. The premise of the show is that in every generation, there is one figure born of the light and one of the darkness – one of God and one of the devil, if you will.

According to Tom, "Carnivale is set during the Depression and has all this fantastic rich texture. Watching the show, we see what the good guy is doing and what the bad guy is doing, all leading up to their eventual meeting at the carnival."

"Anyway," he continues, "There are dark forces in play. And for every yin, there is a yang. The character that represents the light realizes that if he heals one thing, something else is going to die. If he heals one guy's compound-fractured arm, it will probably kill all the fish in the nearby pond. What does he do? For someone to live, someone else must die, and for every good deed, something else must take place…"

In one scene, for example, a character named Brother Justin walks into the middle of a crowded street on a hot summer evening. The next thing he knows, the street, which just a moment ago was packed with people, becomes deserted, and it starts to snow. All of a sudden, something wet hits his face. When he touches his face to wipe it away, he realizes it's blood. Then a drop of blood hits his hand, then a drop hits the street. Now it's raining blood.

"The character realizes it must be a huge sign from God," says Bellissimo. "If one minute he's on a busy city street on a summer night, and then suddenly he's all alone in the snow, and then it starts raining blood, he knows it's not just the weather. It has to be a sign from above – God is trying to tell him something really important. As he stands there contemplating this, the neon sign he's absent-mindedly looking at explodes. As it rips apart, sparks fly, showering him. Following the explosion, the only thing left on the sign is a red cross. He takes this as a sign from a higher spirit telling him something is about to happen."

And in the final frame, isn't that what we love about TV shows and movies? In the movies and on TV, all the playing cards of life are shuffled, flicked up in the air and pouf! They magically fall into some sort of perfect order we might never in a million years have imagined on our own. On screen the random, the chaotic, the tragic and the inexplicable somehow make sense. And give us hope…

Hope that in the movies of our lives, some great unseen hand is running the projector… Hope that in the theater, with disbelief suspended, somehow the darkness and the light, good and evil, all balance out, and some higher power, benevolent after all, really is ultimately in charge of the ending.

Acknowledgments

Thank you to all the below-the-line workers from IATSE Local 44 and Teamsters Local 399 who opened your hearts to me and contributed to this book—and for all your contributions to great television and film; to Shed Behar, for taking a chance on a new writer all those years ago; and to Christina Welsh, for passing me the baton, showing me the ropes, and being a caring, supportive friend and colleague throughout the years since. You started me on the road to becoming a biographer.

Heartfelt appreciation and love to my family, extended family, and friends for your loving companionship and support. And very special thanks to my friend, Former IATSE Local 44 President, John Villarino, for all you contributed to this book.

My deep appreciation to my first publisher, Wayne Orkin (Edee Rose Publishing); to book designer Sue Chidester and book consultant/friend, Flo Selfman, for all you did the first time around; to Ben Ohmart/Bear Manor, for giving this book a second life and giving me a chance to have a second title with your wonderful publishing house; and to John Teehan for your creative design work on this reissue. I know that if my dad (Special Effects Tech, Larry Needham) were still alive today, he'd be smiling to see this book back in print.

Index

1000 Pieces of Gold, 44
12 O'Clock High, 155
"3rd Rock From the Sun," 22
5 Card Stud, 202
A.I., 156
Academy Award Nominations, 2, 72, 159, 176, 185, 197
Academy of Science Fiction, Fantasy & Horror Films, USA – Saturn Award Nominations, 159, 185
Adaptation, 31
Ahrens, Anne, 43
Airport, 90
Airport 77, 155
"Alias," 54, 82
Allard, Eric, 185-187
Allen, Woody, 25, 85, 114-117, 134
Ambrose, Scott, 64-65, 183-184
American Beauty, 16, 171
American Film Institute, 29
American History X, 173-174
Amodio, Angelo M., 56
Analyze That, 176
Anderson, Ira, 93
Anderson, Pamela, 57
Andrea Gail, 157
"Angel," 25
Anna and the King, 141-144
Ann-Margret, 202

Ants, 192
Antunez, James (Jimmy), 18-20
Antunez, Michael, ix, 18-20
"Any Day Now," 64, 123-129, 183
Arachnophobia, 112
Arau, Alfonso, 25-26, 30, 114, 117, 119-121, 134
Ariel Award (Mexico) Nominations, 119
Armageddon, 159, 197
Army of Darkness, 37, 39
As Good as It Gets, 157, 165
ASEPO (Association of Special Effects and Pyrotechnics Coordinators), 149
August, Gina, 48
Autry, Gene, 189
Baby, Secret of the Lost Legend, 32
Bacall, Lauren, 150
Back To The Future II and *III,* 132
Bad Girls, 35
Bad Santa, 109, 166
BAFTA Film Award Nominations, 159
Bancroft, Anne, 3
Barbarians at the Gate, 72
Barnes, Guy, 36
Barnes, Pancho, 194
Basinger, Kim, 55
Batman, 29, 191

Bays, Toby,   45
"Baywatch,"   56
Beaches,   2, 66
Beatty, Warren,   191
Beck, Ty,   143
Beetlejuice,   197-198
Behar, Shed,   218
Belardinelli, Charles "Charlie,"   79-81, 174, 215
Belgrave, Michael,   46-47
Bell, Bradley,   181
Bellissimo, T. Brooklyn "Tom,"   80, 173-175, 215, 219
Beloved,   73
Ben Hur,   155
Benchley, Peter,   97
Bennetts, Bonnie,   43-45
Berkeley, Mowbray "Bunny,"   192
Berry, Kelly,   29-30, 117-118
Bevacqua, Joe,   179-180
"Beverly Hills 90210,"   6, 75
"Bewitched,"   xx, 92, 95, 206, 209, 232
Birds, The,   197-198
Blade,   12
Blue Fairy,   83
Blue Streak,   18
Bobbitt, Scott,   177
"Bold and the Beautiful, The,"   181
"Bonanza,"   189, 191, 201
Bond, Ward,   100
"Boom!"   215
Borgnine, Ernest,   190
Boy Called Hate, A,   57, 59, 171
Brainstorm,   185
Brandy,   54
Break, The,   168

Breaking Point,   168
Brendel, Frank,   137
Brother Justin,   216
"Brutally Normal,"   7-8, 51
"Buffy The Vampire Slayer,"   25
Bugsy,   10
Burella, Tony, Sr.,   20
Burr, Raymond,   191
Burton, Tim,   166, 198
California State University, Northridge,   25, 55
California Suite,   3
Calistro, Paddy,   218
Call of the Wild, The,   192
Campbell, Ray,   xx
Campos, Marco,   138
Cannery Row,   125
Captain Horatio Hornblower R.N.,   192
Cardenas, Robert, Jr.,   69-71
Carey, Drew,   83
Carmichael, Katie,   5
"Carnivale,"   79, 173, 215-216
Carr, Jackie,   112-113, 146
Castaway,   30
Castle, William,   87
CBS Radio,   233
CBS Television City,   16, 51, 95
Chaplin, Charlie,   ix, 18
Chase, The,   92, 206, 232
Cherokee Kid, The,   36
"Chicago Hope,"   164
"CHIPS,"   20
Cider House Rules, The,   ix, 176-177
Cinderella,   54
Cinderella,   xiii, 76

Cinemax, 213
City Slickers 2, 59
Clark, Jason, 186
Clear and Present Danger, 110
Cleveland Institute of Art, 29
"Colby's, The," 56
Color of Money, The, 72
Color Purple, The, 156
"Coma Bar, The," 139
Como Agua para Chocolate, 119
Con Air, 107-108
Confessions of a Dangerous Mind, 25
Connors, Chuck, 174
Conrack, 205
Cooper, Dorree, 120
Cooper, Fred, 179-180
Cooper, Gary, 193
Cordova, Denis, 89
Costner, Kevin, 51
Courage Under Fire, 110
Court-Martial of Billy Mitchell, The, 192
Cowboys, The, 205
Crimson Tide, 18
Crosby, Bing, 196
"CSI: Miami," 101
Culver Studios, 155
Cunningham, Ronnie, 218
"Cybill," 22-23
D'Amico, Gary, 31-33
Dalton, Laurie C., 5-6, 75-77
Dancing at the Harvest Moon, 61
"Dark Shadows," 50
Daughter of the Streets, 56
Davis, Stanford, 12-15

Day of the Dolphins, 12
Daytime Emmy Award Nominations, 179, 181
"Death's Office," 139
Deaton, Gary, 157-158
DeLaurentiis, Dino, 137
Delgado, Vic, 86
Dennis, Eric, 64
DePue, Jim, 57-60
Desantis, Steve, 127-129
DeSantis, Vince, 128
Desilu, 84
Desperado, 174
Devil's Advocate, 144
"Dharma and Greg," 163-164
Dick Tracy, 191
Dietrich, Marlene, 155
Diller, Barry, 3
Disney, 25, 32, 54
Disneyland, 196
"Division, The," 34, 84, 114, 136
Doctor, The, 132
Dogma, 79
Dolan, Charles E. "Chuck," 149-153
Donelan, Tim, 146
Dracula, 2-3, 66
"Dream On," 44
Dude, Where's My Car, 52, 61-62
"Dukes of Hazzard, The," 23
Dumb and Dumberer: When Harry Met Lloyd, 173
Dusk 'Til Dawn, 174
Dutton, Tim, 23
Dykstra, John, 186
"Dynasty," 56
E.T., 112, 146, 156

Eagles,   155
Earhart, Amelia,   194
Eastwood, Clint,   198
Effner, Ryan,   9-11, 52-53
Electric Horseman, The,   125
Emmy Award Nominations,   2, 22, 37, 72
Employee of the Month,   127
Endangered Species,   171
Erin Brockovich,   ix, 131
Ernest, Orien,   137
Evening Star,   144
"Everybody Loves Raymond,"   116
Fabulous Baker Boys, The,   40-41
"Falcon Crest,"   191
"Fame,"   171
"Family Affair,"   85
"Family,"   56
Fargo,   87-88
Farrell, Mike,   101
Fasano, Luigi "Lou,"   189-191
Fat Man and Little Boy,   120
"Father Murphy,"   169
"Felicity,"   7-8, 54, 82
Fields, W.C.,   196
Fight Club,   172
Flynn, Errol,   193
Ford, Harrison,   72
Forrestel, Jack,   181
Fraser, Brendan,   105, 112
Frazier, John,   159-162
Freaky Friday,   138
Free Willy,   10, 125
Freiburger, Eugene "Geno,"   40-42
Freitas, Walter,   12
Fresco, Mike,   36, 76

Frey, Glenn,   155
"From the Earth to the Moon,"   37
Fun with Dick and Jane,   2, 66
G.I. Jane,   141, 144
Gaffin, Lauri,   87-88
Galvin, Glen,   99
Garfield,   29, 117
Garland, Beverly,   xii, 219
Gaspar, Chuck,   197-199
Gaspar, Geeza,   197
Gaynor, Mitzi,   150
General's Daughter, The,   107-108, 110
George of the Jungle,   28
Gepetto,   2, 16-17, 66, 82-83
Gepetto,   ix, 83
Gere, Richard,   55
Ghostbusters,   197-198
Ghostbusters II,   198
Giorgianni, Joseph,   139
Glory Days,   27
Glory,   2-3, 66
Godfather, The,   155
Godzilla,   138
Golden Satellite Award Nominations,   159, 185
Gone in Sixty Seconds,   46-47
Goonies, The,   131
Goss, Joe,   137
Graveyard Shift,   10
Great Race, The,   192
Greatest Story Ever Told, The,   204-205
Greener Mountains,   5
Gremlins,   112
"Guardian, The,"   171

Guilty as Charged, 84, 136
Hafemann, Alan, 205
Hafemann, Frank, 204-205
Hallelujah Trail, The, 205
Hallmark Hall of Fame, 35
"Hammer, The," 169
Hampton, Larry, 197
Handyman's Union Local 42, 7
Hanson, Sydney, 76
Hard Target, 39
Harper, Clyde, 169-170, 200-203
Hartigan, John, 16-17
Hatfield, Walt, 90
Haugen, Keith, 102
Haunting of Seacliff Inn, The, 181
Hawaii, 205
HBO, 36, 51, 215-216
Hedren, Tippi, 198
Hello Dolly, 3
Hennessy, Michael, 219
Herbie, 32
Herbie Goes Bananas, 32
Herman, Pee Wee, 199
"Highway to Heaven," 169, 200-201
Hoffman, Richard, 219
Hoffmann, David, 179
Holes, 50
Home for the Holidays, 185
"Home Improvement," 132-133
Honey, I Shrunk the Kids, 120
Hook, 2, 4, 66
Hope, Bob, 196
House on Haunted Hill, The, 79, 87
"How Green Was My Valley," 163
"Huff," 37, 64, 183

Hultstrom, Bill, 179
Hunter, Bobby, 59
"Huntress, The," 37-39, 46, 56
Hurt, William, 132
I Am Sam, 2, 66
"I Dream of Jeannie," xx
I.A.T.S.E. (International Association of Theater and Stage Employees), 86
I.A.T.S.E. Local 18, 40
I.A.T.S.E. Local 44, 89, , 140, 142, 149, 154, 208, 214
If Men Could Talk, 11
Imax, 213
Immortal, The, 202
In Good Company, 16
"In Living Color," 69
Incorvaia, Carl, 137
Incredible Shrinking Woman, 210
Independence Day, 138, 139
Industrial Light & Magic, 160
Interceptor, 43
International Alliance of Theatrical and Stage Employees (I.A.T.S.E.), xviii
Interpreter, The, 176
"Iron Horse, The," xix, 95, 208, 232
"Ironside," 191
Island, The, 54, 82, 97, 206
Italian Job, The, 29, 117
Jack Klugman, Jack, 155
"Jack of All Trades," 168-169, 171
Jack the Bear, 163
Jackson, Courtney, 25-26
Jackson, Mary Ann, 149
Jane Austen's Mafia, 46-47
Jaws, xx, 92, 97, 115, 136, 206, 210, 232

Jaws 2, 92, 206, 232
Jaws 4, 92, 206, 232
Joel, Andrea, 179-180
Johnny Be Good, 120
Johnson, George Clayton, 219, 233
Jurassic Park, 89-90, 112, 127, 146, 154, 156
"Just Shoot Me," 40-41, 43-44
Karz, Mike, 82
Kasden, Larry, 166
Kaye, Danny, 145
Kennedy, John F., 152
Kersey, John, ix, 101-103
Kersey, John, Sr., 103
KHJ, 40
King Kong, 115, 136-137
Kintzer, Cortney, 219
Kitchen, Butch, 64
Klimt, Gustav, 54
Klinesmith, Gene, 51
Klopp, Kathy, 43
"Knight Rider," 95-96, 232
Knight, Roger, 45
Kodak, 11
Kooper, Vivien, 232-233
Kosnett, James, 218
Krakoff, Gary, 138-140
Krakoff, Gary, Jr., 139
Lafferty, Tim, 139
Lancer, Bob, 219
Landon, Michael, 169-170, 191, 201
"Las Vegas," 112, 146
Last Flight of Noah's Ark, The, 32
Last Samurai, The, 109
Leachman, Cloris, 23, 69
"Leaving L.A.," 183

Legally Blonde 2: Red, White & Blonde, 27
Legan, Mark, 70
Lemmon, Jack, 202
Leno, Jay, 59
Leroy, Ed, 86
Lethal Weapon, 87
Level 9, 51
Lewis, Garrett, 2-4, 66-68
Liberty Stands Still, 12
Life of the Party: The Pamela Harriman Story, 183
Life of the Party: The Pamela Harriman Story, 64
Like Water For Chocolate, 114, 119-120
"Little House on The Prairie," 169, 201
Little House: Bless All the Dear Children, 200
Local 399, xviii, 8, 168, 195, 200-201, 214
Logan's Run, 108, 233
Lomax, John, III, 219
Lombardi, Paul, 109-111
Los Invisibles, 135
Louis-Dreyfuss, Julia, 83
"Love is a Many Splendored Thing," 163
Love Me Tender, 163
Lucas, Bob, 118
"Lucy Show, The," 204
Lynch, David, 32
"M*A*S*H," 101, 163
"Mad About You," 40-41
"Make Room For Daddy," 190
Malick, Wendie, 44

Mancinelli, Mark, 143
"Mannix," 85, 205
Mantegna, Joe, 25
Marooned, 206
"Married with Children," 69-70
Mars Attacks, 138
Martin, Dean, 189, 202
Masius, John, 76
Mask, The, 79, 174
Mason, Scott, 143
Master and Commander: The Far Side of the World, 157
Matilda, 43
Maxwell, Ray, 134-135
McCartney, Paul, 155
McCrae, Kent, 169-170
"McHale's Navy," 189-190
McIntosh, Mary Olivia, 124-126
Mendoza, Sammy, 139
Metal God, 20
MGM Studios, 132, 149, 168, 192, 197
Michener, James, 205
Minority Report, 89, 154
Miriam Titlebaum, Homocide, 46
Missing, The, 34
"Mission Impossible," 85, 205
Mitchum, Robert, 202
Moguls, The, 79
Monkey Bone, 27, 105-113, 138-139, 178
Monroe, Marilyn, 196
"Moonlighting," 102, 149
Moore, Lee, 181
Moore, Tom, 82
Moser, Rochelle, ix, 22-24
Moss, Monique, 219

Mr. Murder, 35
MTV, 173
Mulholland Drive, 32
Mumford, 178
Muppet Movie, The, 16, 108
"Murder She Wrote," 55
Music Within, The, 119
My Fair Lady, 3
"My Favorite Martian," xx
"My So-Called Life," 5-6, 75-76
"Nanny, The," 41
Needham, Lawrence "Larry," x, ix, xix, 92-100, 206-211, 219, 232
Nelson, Kristen, 23
Never Been Kissed, 48
Never Too Young to Die, 9, 52
New Line Cinema, 10
"New WKRP in Cincinnati, The" 22
Nickloff, Loren, ix, 131-133
Nickolaides, Steve, 59
Nightmare On Elm Street 4, 10
Nightmare On Elm Street: The Dream Child, A, 9-10, 52, 81
Nine Lives, 25
Nixon, 166-167
No Mercy, 55
Norrbom, Bruce, 139
Nurse Betty, 61
O'Hara, Karen, 72-74
O'Hara, Kathleen, 44
O'Neal, Ryan, 202
O'Neal, Tatum, 202
O'Toole, Annette, 46
Ocean's 11, 233
Old Man And the Sea, The, 192
Olmos, Edward James, 25

Olson, Milt, 86
Once in a Lifetime, 101
Online Film Critics Society Award Nominations, 160
Orkin, Wayne, 218
"Our Gang," 149
Out of Towners, The, 202
Ozols-Barnes, Wendy, 34-36
Paint Your Wagon, 194, 196
Pale Rider, 198
Panavision, 11
Panic Room, 2, 66, 141
Paper Moon, 200, 202
Paramount Studios, 10, 51, 85-86, 192
Park, Tim, 44
Parshalle, Leanne, 218
PBS, 44
Pearl Harbor, 20, 159
Pee Wee's Big Adventure, 199
Pemberton, Dan, 141-145
Pemberton, Ray, 141
Pentecost, Jim, 82
Perfect Storm, The, 157, 159, 160-161, 166-167
Petrotta, William "Bill," 166-167
Pettibone, Doug, 137
Pfeiffer, Michelle, 72, 80
Piccone, Jimmy, 143
Picking Up The Pieces, 25-26, 30, 84, 114-122, 134, 136
Pinocchio, 66-67, 82-83
Pizzini, Denise, ix, 118-122
Pleasantville, ix, 18
Plym, Stephen M., 233
Polito, Jennifer, 43
Postman, The, 51

Poulik, Michele, 37-39
Poynton, Cyril, 194-196
Presley, Elvis, 163
Pretty Woman, 4
Price, Vincent, 87, 145
Producer's Studios, 86
"Providence," 31, 34-36, 75-77, 101-102
Pryor, Richard, 7-8
Psycho (remake), 29, 117
PT-109, 152
"Quantum Leap," 41
Quincy, M.D., 89
"Quincy, M.D.," 90, 155
Radaelli, Chip, 35
Raise the Titanic, 16
Raleigh Studios, 86
Rami, Sam, 39
Ransom of Red Chief, The, 36
"Rat Pack," 189
Rayve, Abby, 41
Reagan, Ronald, 189
Redford, Robert, 92
Reed, Leo, 214
"Remington Steele," 22-23
Republic Pictures, 189
Rescue Me, 56
Reseigne, Dick, 107
Rhoades, Arthur S. "Art," 192-193
Rio Bravo, 205
Riva, Michael, 155
Robertson, Dale, 96
Robinson, Edward G., 193
Robinson, Glen, 137
Rogers, Roy, 189
Romy and Michele's High School Reunion, 134

Ross, Herbert, 3
Roth, John, 84-86, 136
"Route 66," 196
Rubino, Beth, ix, 176-178
Rules of Attraction, The, 166
Rumble Fish, 125
Rush, Geoffrey, 87
Russo, 51
SAG, 11, 32
San Antonio Film Commission, 120
Saved by the Bell:Wedding in Las Vegas, 69
"Scarecrow and Mrs. King," 116
Scheide, Charlotte Garnell, 181-182
Schultz, Al, 194
Schwanke, David, 168-171
Schwanke, Paul, 168, 171-172
Schwartz, Todd David, 219, 233
Schwarzenegger, Arnold, 144
Scott, David L., ix, 54-55, 82-83
Scott, Ridley, 144
Scott, Sue Chidester, 218
Sealy, Cheryl, 218
Segal, George, 41
Selfman, Flo, 218
Serling, Rod, xx
Serna, Pepe, 85
Serrano, Charlie, 139
She's All That, 9, 52
Shenandoah, 155
Shepard, Cybill, 102
"Shield, The," 37
Short Circuit 2, 185
Short Circuit, 185
Shrink Is In, The, 62
Siege, 110

Silence of the Lambs, The, 72
Silver, Joel, 87
Sinatra, Frank, 189-190
Slatsky, John, 146
Sleepers, 178
"Sliders," 55, 59, 114, 116, 136
Slonecker, Bill, 143
"Smoke Through My Fingers," 233
Some Like it Hot, 194, 196
Something Wicked This Way Comes, 32
Sonny & Cher, 196
Sons of Katie Elder, The, 202
Sony Studios, 73, 185
"Sopranos, The," 51
South Pacific, 150
Spade, David, 41
Sparkle Films, 39
Special Effects Unlimited, 186
Speed, 159
Spelling, Aaron, 56
Spider-Man, 72, 159-160
Spider-Man 2, 159-160
Spielberg, Stephen, 146, 156
Spike TV, 215
Spy Kids, 185
Star Trek 9, 48
"Star Trek," 85, 204
Star Wars, 3
Stark, Ray, 3
Stewart, Chuck, 107-109
Stewart, Jimmy, 155
Stone, Oliver, 166
Stone, Sharon, 85, 114, 116, 144
Storaro, Vittorio, 121
Straight Story, The, 32

Straight, Alvin,   32
Streisand, Barbra,   3
Stuart Little,   185, 186
Stuntman's Association,   51
"Superman,"   191
Surkin, Eddie,   84, 86, 114-116, 136-137
Sutton, Phoef,   69
Swingers,   202
"Tales From the Crypt,"   174
Tarzan,   37, 94
Taylor, Michael,   35
TBS,   48
Texas Films,   189
Texas Tech University,   120
"Thanks,"   23, 69, 131
"That '80s Show,"   5, 75
Thin Red Line, The,   166
"Third Rock From The Sun,"   23
Thomas, Danny,   190
Thorson, Dottie,   38-39
Thorson, Ralph "Papa,"   38
Thou Shalt Not Kill Except,   39
"Threat Matrix,"   124
"Time Cop,"   59
Tiny Tim and Mr. Plym: Life As We Knew It,   233
Titanic,   84
Titanic (the original),   189
Tollbooth,   168
Tomashoff, Sy,   181
Torpin, Randy,   163-164
Total Recall,   144
"Townies,"   124
Tracy, Spencer,   193
Traffic,   149
Trespass,   131

Trevino, Dave,   143
Tron,   32
Turk, Daniel,   61-62
Turning Point, The,   3
Tuttle, Bart,   193
Twentieth Century Fox,   150
Twentieth Century Fox Ranch,   163
Twilight Zone, the Movie,   146, 178
"Twilight Zone, The,"   xx, 104, 233
Twister,   50, 159, 161, 197
Ubick, Chris,   27-28
UCLA,   31, 99
United Artists,   192
Universal Studios,   xx, 22, 31, 59, 77, 90, 101, 103, 155, 171, 189, 197, 206,
University of Illinois,   74
USC,   99
U-Turn,   166
"V.I.P.,"   48, 57, 59
Van Dyke, Rob,   89
Vanilla Sky,   31
Variety,   86
Verdick, Jeff,   50-51
Videla, Gabe,   186
Villarino, John,   89-91, 154, 156, 214, 219
Villarino, Mike,   89
Vista Vision,   213-214
Visual Effects Society Award Nominations,   79, 160, 173
"Wackiest Ship in the Army, The,"   92
Waddell, Jimmy,   219, 233
Waff, Freddy,   45
Walk in the Clouds, A,   119
Walker, Justin,   143
Warner Brothers,   3, 48, 157, 190-192

Warner, Jack, 193
Warren Cowan Associates, 219
Waterworld, 91, 144
Wayne, John, 99, 100, 196, 202, 205
Welsh, Christina, 218
"Werewolf," 174
What Lies Beneath, 72, 79-80, 89-90, 154, 173-174
White Men Can't Jump, 12
White, E.B., 186
Why Do Fools Fall in Love, 134
Willis, Bruce, 102
Winters, Jonathan, 145
"Without a Trace," 57, 127
Witness, 149
Wizard of Oz, The, 194, 196
Wonderful Ice Cream Suit, The, 25
Woo, John, 39
Wood, Natalie, 185, 205
Wyatt, Monica, 76
Wyman, Jane, 191
X-Files, The, 107
"X-Files," 163-164
xXx, 159
"Young and the Restless, The," 179
Young, Loretta, 193
Zanuck, Darryl, 164
Zapata, Pedro, 7-8
Zathura, 87
Zemeckis, Robert, 146, 174

About the Author

Vivien Cooper is a native of Los Angeles who also spent seven wonderful years in Nashville, Tennessee. She is the daughter of the late mechanical special effects technician, Larry Needham (Bewitched, Knight Rider, The Iron Horse, *The Chase, Jaws 1, 2* and *4, etc.)*

One of the highlights of her childhood was the day her dad arranged for her to spend the day on set with Rod Serling. As fate would have it, she would later meet many of her film, T.V., and musical heroes, as well.

Vivien is an author, poet, song lyricist, biographer, and speech writer. She is the author of *George Clayton Johnson: Fictioneer*

(Bear Manor Media 2013), and the writer of *The Instrumental Alphabet* spoken word CD (with Grammy winning keyboardist, Brother Paul Brown).

The author lives in L.A., practices her Episcopal faith, and looks for the highest good in all things. When she is not writing, listening to music, wandering around the museum, or spending time with loved ones, she can often be found at the movies or watching great T.V. shows.

www.ingramcontent.com/pod-product-compliance
Lightning Source LLC
Chambersburg PA
CBHW071426150426
43191CB00008B/1059